SCIENTIFIC AMERICAN EXPLORES BIG IDEAS

Understanding Autism Spectrum Disorder

Published in 2024 by Scientific American Educational Publishing
in association with **The Rosen Publishing Group**
2544 Clinton Street, Buffalo NY 14224

Contains material from Scientific American®, a division of Springer Nature America, Inc., reprinted by permission, as well as original material from The Rosen Publishing Group®.

First Edition

Scientific American
Lisa Pallatroni: Project Editor

Rosen Publishing
Daniel R. Faust : Compiling Editor
Michael Moy: Senior Graphic Designer

Cataloging-in-Publication Data

Names: Scientific American, Inc.
Title: Understanding autism spectrum disorder / edited by the Scientific American Editors.
Description: New York : Scientific American Educational Publishing, 2024. |
Series: Scientific American explores big ideas | Includes glossary and index.
Identifiers: ISBN 9781725349452 (pbk.) | ISBN 9781725349469
(library bound)| ISBN 9781725349476 (ebook)
Subjects: LCSH: Autism spectrum disorders.
Classification: LCC RC553.A88 U534 2024 | DDC 616.85'882-dc23

Manufactured in the United States of America
Websites listed were live at the time of publication.

Cover: SewCreamStudio/Shutterstock.com

CPSIA Compliance Information: Batch # SACS24.
For Further Information contact Rosen Publishing at 1-800-237-9932.

CONTENTS

INTRODUCTION

In 2021, the Centers for Disease Control and Prevention (CDC) reported that approximately 1 in 44 children in the United States has been diagnosed with an autism spectrum disorder (ASD). Autism spectrum disorder refers to a diverse group of conditions related to brain development. ASD is characterized by difficulties with social interaction and communication, as well as atypical patterns of behavior. Although often diagnosed in childhood, the wide range of behaviors associated with autism spectrum disorder means that many children may go undiagnosed until much later in life, if at all.

The articles in this book have been selected in order to provide a better understanding of autism spectrum disorder, as well as those who have been diagnosed with ASD. Section 1, "What Is Autism Spectrum Disorder?" offers an introduction to ASD and looks at some of the issues behind early attempts to identify and understand it. Section 2, "Detection and Diagnosis," examines some of the latest research in the ways that ASD is detected in children and adults. Special attention is given to the need for better methods of detection among certain groups, like women. Section 3, "What Causes Autism Spectrum Disorder?" attempts to remove some of the mystery surrounding the causes of autism spectrum disorder. Common misconceptions about autism and neurodiversity are also examined in the articles found in this section. Section 4, "Life on the Spectrum," offers a glimpse into the day-to-day life of individuals diagnosed with ASD. Articles shine a light on both the struggle and the potential of people with autism spectrum disorder. Section 5, "Myths and Misconceptions," looks at the negative effects that common misconceptions and misunderstandings have on the ASD community, including the harmful assumption that autism spectrum disorder is something that needs to be "cured."

Section 1: What Is Autism Spectrum Disorder?

A New Idea That Could Help Us Understand Autism

By Pamela Feliciano

As social beings, when thinking about autism we tend to focus on its social challenges, such as difficulty communicating, making friends and showing empathy. I am a geneticist and the mother of a teenage boy with autism. I too worry most about whether he'll have the conversational skills to do basic things like grocery shopping or whether he will ever have a real friend. But I assure you that the nonsocial features of autism are also front and center in our lives: intense insistence on sameness, atypical responses to sensory stimuli and a remarkable ability to detect small details. Many attempts have been made to explain all the symptoms of autism holistically, but no one theory has yet explained all the condition's puzzling and diverse features.

Now, a growing number of neurocognitive scientists think that many traits found in people with autism spectrum disorder (ASD) may be explained centrally by impairments in predictive skills—and have begun testing this hypothesis.

Generally, the human brain determines what's coming next based on the status quo, plus what we recall from previous experiences. Scientists theorize that people with ASD have differences that disturb their ability to predict. It's not that people with autism can't make predictions; it's that their predictions are flawed because they perceive the world "too accurately." Their predictions are less influenced by prior experiences and more influenced by what they are experiencing in the moment. They overemphasize the "now."

When the connections between an event and a consequence are very clear, people with ASD can learn them. But the real world is an ever-changing environment with a lot of complexity and sometimes contingencies and deviations are as not as obvious. Many individuals with autism have difficulty figuring out which cues are most important, because there are too many other cues complicating the environment and competing for attention.

Five years ago, the Simons Foundation's autism research initiative launched SPARK (Simons Powering Autism Research for Knowledge) to harness the power of big data by engaging hundreds of thousands of individuals with autism and their family members to participate in research. The more people who participate, the deeper and richer these data sets become, catalyzing research that is expanding our knowledge of both biology and behavior to develop more precise approaches to medical and behavioral issues. Scientists are now recruiting SPARK participants to study directly observable aspects of prediction more closely. There are two components that can be observed: the ability to learn the connection between an "antecedent" event and its consequence, and responses to predictable events.

Pawan Sinha of MIT recently published results from a study showing that people with ASD had very different responses to a highly regular sequence of tones played on a metronome than those without ASD. While people without ASD "habituate" to the sequence of regular tones; people with ASD do not acclimate to the sounds over time. Rather, their responses after several minutes of hearing the tone sequence were still as robust as they were when they were first played. Using SPARK's powerful digital platform, Sinha and colleagues are now able to conduct similar experiments online with a much larger number of people with autism.

As the researchers acknowledge, the connections between the decreased habituation and real-world challenges in people with autism are still not clear, but testing multiple aspects of prediction in more naturalistic contexts in a larger number of people will help address that knowledge gap. Eventually, a better understanding of the cognitive processes in autism may help to improve interventions–for example, by tailoring different prediction-based interventions to individuals with varying prediction styles.

Every parent of a teenager has their share of challenges, and, for me, an ongoing issue for my son is that he really seems to enjoy engaging in behaviors that will elicit a response from someone. Some of these "habits" have small consequences. For example, he loves to empty entire bottles of soap, detergent, and cooking oil. He also likes to throw things out of his window. More than once, I've been out walking the dog and noticed pants on the roof of our house.

While one cannot deny the satisfaction inherent in dumping a lot of fine olive oil into a drain, it's impossible for me to ever fully understand why my son does any of these things. Still, I have a strong suspicion it's because he knows these behaviors will elicit a predictable response from me. I have learned that the more I respond, the more he will be encouraged to behave this way. So, now, when I find an empty bottle of detergent in the laundry room—or an entire roll of toilet paper in the bowl—I don't make a big deal of it.

Then comes the test of tests: one of his most problematic behaviors is touching our dog's rear end. He knows he is not supposed to do this. He knows that, likely, someone might gasp aloud and then tell him to wash his hands. If his abilities to predict are impaired, then it makes sense that doing things that elicit predictable responses must be satisfying. Having a scientific framework that helps explain his behaviors helps me cope with them. More importantly, a better understanding increases my empathy for him, helps me explain his actions more clearly to others, and helps me remember not to react strongly.

Scientists are also using SPARK to test other aspects of prediction in autism, including language. Harvard University scientist Jesse Snedeker is recruiting participants from SPARK to test whether children with autism are less likely to make accurate predictions during natural language comprehension of simple sentences. These experiments will explore if children with autism differ in using linguistic context to predict upcoming words when hearing a story or conversation. The results will help scientists learn whether impairments in prediction in different people with autism are more broad or more specific to different domains.

As a parent and a researcher, my greatest hope is to help moms like me, children like Dylan, and families like mine. The challenges of understanding autism are many, but a better understanding of predictive patterns in autism will help us all—researchers and families—understand the many "whys" that remain a hallmark of autism.

This is an opinion and analysis article; the views expressed by the author or authors are not necessarily those of Scientific American.

About the Author

Pamela Feliciano, Ph.D., is the scientific director of SPARK (Simons Foundation Powering Autism Research through Knowledge) and is a senior scientist at SFARI (Simons Foundation Autism Research Initiative). SPARK is a SFARI initiative that seeks to accelerate autism research through a vibrant and informative online platform that meaningfully engages individuals with autism spectrum disorder (ASD) and their families and connects them to interested researchers.

By the Numbers: Autism Is Not a Math Problem

By Ferris Jabr

At a meeting of the Icelandic Medical Association last week, Yale University child psychologist Fred Volkmar gave a presentation on how the American Psychiatric Association (APA) is changing the definition of autism. In his talk, Volkmar came to a startling conclusion: more than half of the people who meet the existing criteria for autism would not meet the APA's new definition of autism and, therefore, may not receive state educational and medical services.

The APA defines autism in a reference guide for clinicians called the *Diagnostic and Statistical Manual for Mental Disorders (DSM)*. The newest version of the manual, the *DSM-5*, is slated for publication in May 2013.

In Iceland, Volkmar presented data from an unpublished preliminary analysis of 372 high-functioning autistic children and adults with IQs above 70. He plans to publish a broader analysis later this year. On a key PowerPoint slide that Volkmar shared with *Scientific American*, he notes that there are 2,688 ways to get a diagnosis of autistic disorder in *DSM-IV*, but only six ways to get a diagnosis of autism spectrum disorder in *DSM-5*. Although intriguing at first glance, it turns out that both these numbers are slightly wrong–and that they are pretty much useless when comparing the *DSM-IV* and *DSM-5*. You cannot reduce autism to a math problem.

Scientific American wanted to explore this gaping discrepancy further, so we asked astronomer and Hubble Fellow Joshua Peek of Columbia University to code a computer program that would calculate the total possible ways to get a diagnosis of autistic disorder in *DSM-IV* and the total possible ways to get a diagnosis of autism spectrum disorder in *DSM-5*. You can do the math by hand, too, if you like: It all comes down to factorials. The *DSM-IV* criteria are a set of 12 items in three groups from which you must choose 6, with at least two items from group one and at least one item each from groups two and three. The *DSM-5* criteria are a set of seven items in two groups from which you must choose five, including all three items in group one and at least two of the four items in group two. Peek's program crunched the numbers: there are 2,027 different ways to be diagnosed with autism in *DSM-IV* and 11 ways to be diagnosed with autism in *DSM-5*.

One might think that those statistics make it absurdly easy to qualify for a diagnosis of autism in *DSM-IV* and incredibly difficult to meet the criteria for autism in *DSM-5*, but those numbers alone don't tell you anything unless you understand how common each symptom of autism is in the general population. Symptoms of autism are not randomly distributed throughout the population and the symptoms do not cluster together in random combinations. Research in the past decade has shown that some symptoms appear together much more often than others. In fact, that is one of the main reasons that the APA has consolidated the *DSM-IV* criteria for autism into fewer, denser and more accurate criteria in the *DSM-5*. The idea is that the *DSM-IV* criteria allowed for too many possible combinations, many of which rarely occur; the *DSM-5* criteria, in contrast, better reflect the most common combinations of symptoms.

Specifically, the APA has merged two distinct groups of symptoms from the *DSM-IV*—deficits in communication and deficits in social interaction—into one group in the *DSM-5* because someone with autism almost always has both kinds of symptoms.

Most psychiatrists applaud this consolidation because, as several recently published studies have shown, the new criteria are more precise: they rarely assign autism to people who do not have it. However, the *DSM-5* criteria may be a little too strict, ignoring some autistic people with milder symptoms. Two recently published studies suggest an easy fix: if the new criteria require that patients meet one fewer symptom—four out of seven instead of five out of seven—high-functioning autistic people will not be excluded.

About the Author

Ferris Jabr is a contributing writer for Scientific American. *He has also written for the* New York Times Magazine, *the* New Yorker *and* Outside.

The Problem with Asperger's

By Edith Sheffer

Millions of people are identified with Asperger's syndrome, as a diagnosis, an identity and even an adjective. Asperger's name has permeated our culture—yet I believe we should no longer invoke it.

Naming medical diagnoses after individuals is an honor, meant to recognize those who discover conditions and to commend their work. While there is a move toward descriptive diagnostic labels in medicine, certain eponyms have entered our everyday language and will likely endure. Alzheimer's and Parkinson's diseases, for example.

Hans Asperger, however, neither described Asperger syndrome as we understand it today nor merits commendation. I have spent seven years researching his past in Nazi Vienna, uncovering his complicity in the Nazi regime and its "euthanasia" program that murdered children considered to be disabled. Contrary to Asperger's reputation as a resister in the Third Reich, he approved the transfer of dozens of children to Vienna's killing center, Spiegelgrund, where they perished. He publicly spoke—and published—about the need to send the most "difficult cases" to Spiegelgrund. He was also close colleagues with top euthanasia figures in Vienna, including Erwin Jekelius, the director of Spiegelgrund, who was engaged to Hitler's sister.

Nazi ideology shaped Asperger's research. Children in the Third Reich were to display community spirit, being enthusiastic participants in collective activities such as the Hitler youth. In Germany in the 1930s, Nazi psychiatrists identified children whom they believed lacked social feeling, unable to join the national community. Asperger, in his early 30s, warned against classifying children, arguing that they should be regarded as individuals. But right after the Third Reich annexed Austria in 1938—and the purge of his Jewish and liberal associates from the University of Vienna—Asperger followed his senior colleagues in Nazi child psychiatry and introduced his own diagnosis of social detachment: "autistic psychopathy."

The term psychopathy carried criminal connotations in Nazi child psychiatry, and indeed Asperger attributed "sadistic" traits to autistic children. His definition of the diagnosis grew harsher year after year, as he sought promotion to associate professor under his ardent Nazi mentor, Franz Hamburger. By 1944, while lauding the "highly original genius" of children on the "favorable" end of his autistic "range," he said those on the "unfavorable end" would grow up to "roam the streets as 'originals,' grotesque and dilapidated." He also embraced the fascist rhetoric of Nazi psychiatry, maintaining that autistic children did not fit into "the organism of the social community." In this view, autism was the psychological opposite of Nazism.

In the postwar period, Asperger distanced himself from his Nazi-era work on autistic psychopathy. His work remained little known outside Austria until leading British psychiatrist Lorna Wing discovered Asperger's 1944 thesis and publicized the diagnosis in 1981 as "Asperger's syndrome." The idea took off. In 1992, the World Health Organization included it as a distinct diagnosis in its *International Classification of Diseases*, Tenth Revision (*ICD-10*), and in 1994, the American Psychiatric Association added Asperger's disorder to its *Diagnostic and Statistical Manual of Mental Disorders* (*DSM-IV*). Neither body, it would seem, thoroughly vetted Asperger's life during the Third Reich before giving the diagnosis his name.

The new idea of an autism "spectrum" encompassed many different types of children. Navigating the diagnosis became complicated. In the United States, the broad category of pervasive developmental disorder (PDD) included autism, Asperger's disorder and pervasive developmental disorder not otherwise specified (PDD-NOS). In reality, the lines between the diagnostic criteria were fuzzy. My son, for instance, was diagnosed with all three conditions by three different clinics. There was endless analysis; PDD-NOS was applied as "autism-lite," while Asperger disorder hinged upon whether his speech was sufficiently typical.

While the diagnostic subdivisions of the autism spectrum seemed subjective, the labels had profound real-world consequences. A child diagnosed with autism typically received far more public services and school support than a child diagnosed with Asperger disorder or PDD-NOS. Children with the latter diagnoses often went without the help they needed.

Because of indistinct diagnostic criteria, the American Psychiatric Association reclassified Asperger disorder and PDD-NOS as autism spectrum disorder in 2013. Now, the World Health Organization is poised to do the same in the *International Classification of Diseases*. Losing the Asperger's diagnosis has been controversial, since many identify with Asperger's more than they do with autism, or fear that the spectrum is being narrowed—that some people with needs might not meet the changed criteria for autism and thus go without support.

Personally, I agree with the reclassification of the Asperger's diagnosis. For a psychiatric diagnosis, the subdivisions never made sense for my son, and got in the way of his care. For an eponymous diagnosis, Asperger merits neither the credit nor the honor—and in fact, other conditions named after physicians found to have participated in Nazi extermination now go by other terms, such as Reiter Syndrome (reactive arthritis).

The fact is, autism spectrum disorder remains a vexing, heterogeneous diagnosis. Our psychiatric organizations have left us without a good vocabulary for articulating distinctions among people. In shorthand, professionals and parents may slot people as having "low-functioning," "mid-functioning," or "high-functioning" autism, language that can be problematic. Hopefully, as research progresses, we will develop a more appropriate vocabulary. In the meantime, we can effect a positive change by no longer invoking Asperger's name.

The views expressed are those of the author(s) and are not necessarily those of Scientific American.

Section 2: Detection and Diagnosis

Detecting Autism Early

By Ulrich Kraft

Anyone who has spent even a little time with an autistic boy or girl soon becomes familiar with the behaviors that set these children apart: lack of eye contact, trouble verbalizing, overreacting or underreacting to activities around them, difficulty in expressing their feelings and in understanding the emotions of others. But how do parents and doctors know if a baby, who is too immature to be gauged on any of these traits, has autism? Early diagnosis has proved difficult.

Inability to detect autism until a child is two or three years old is a terrific disadvantage. It "eliminates a valuable window of treatment opportunity, when the brain is undergoing tremendous development," says David G. Amaral, professor of neurobiology and psychiatry at the University of California, Davis.

Amaral and researchers at other institutions, however, are closing in on techniques that could detect autism in babies as young as six months and perhaps even at birth. The results of these new tests–some controversial–are expanding the understanding of autism and raising hopes for much earlier, specialized care that could improve a toddler's chances for a more normal life as a child, teenager and adult.

A Simple Blood Test?

Autism affects a wide variety of developmental traits. Some young autistic children speak; others do not. Some possess almost average intellectual abilities; others are severely limited. As they grow older, certain autistic individuals display incredible talents in very specific domains. Known as savants, they can memorize an entire book in hours or solve complex math problems faster than people using a calculator. The 1988 movie *Rain Man* dramatized these abilities in a character named Raymond Babbitt, played by Dustin Hoffman, who won an Oscar for the role. Babbitt was based on a real savant named Kim Peek, who continues to astonish today.

It is no wonder, then, that determining whether a young child is autistic is fraught with uncertainty. Diagnosis typically involves rating a child's behaviors against a set of standards. The exercise usually is not conclusive until at least the child's second birthday. That is why scientists are seeking an earlier and more accurate test, and they are getting closer. At the International Meeting for Autism Research in Boston in May 2005, Amaral presented the initial results of a landmark study. His team compared blood samples from 70 autistic children ages four to six with samples from 35 randomly selected subjects in the same age group. The autistic children had a higher proportion of two basic immune system cells known as B cells and T cells. Significant differences also became apparent in more than 100 proteins and small molecules commonly found in the bloodstream.

After further analysis, the team decided that the pilot study results were strong enough to launch a full-scale investigation. In March 2006 Amaral announced that U.C. Davis's Medical Investigation of Neurodevelopmental Disorders Institute, which he heads, was starting the Autism Phenome Project. It will enroll 900 children with autism plus 450 more who have developmental delays and 450 who are developing normally. Researchers will analyze the children's blood proteins, immune systems, brain structures and functions, genetics and environmental exposures. The participants will be two to four years old at the outset and will be followed for several years. Amaral thinks it is probable that telltale genetic markers will be found. But it will take several years before the project is finished and analyzed and longer still before a routine test for autism could be administered at a doctor's office.

If the blood profiles prove to be reliable, the screening could occur just after a baby is born. But the validity of detection that early in life requires more scrutiny. Amaral says there is a growing view among experts that not all individuals who have autism are "doomed at birth," as has been commonly believed. "It may be that some children have a vulnerability, such as a genetic abnormality," he says, "and that something they encounter after being born, perhaps in their environment, triggers the disorder."

Environment is suspected in part because the incidence of autism is fairly high in American children. The disorder affects one in every 150 eight-year-olds, according to the latest estimates from the U.S. Centers for Disease Control and Prevention. The unexplained preponderance has frustrated scientists trying to find answers. Furthermore, tremendous variation exists among symptoms, "which leads us to believe that autism is a group of disorders rather than a single disorder–several autisms versus one," Amaral says. The blood work could possibly define distinct subtypes. Behavioral experts are reaching the same conclusion, many preferring the term "autism spectrum disorder" rather than simply "autism."

Earlier Treatment Is Key

An early diagnosis is so important because it would allow treatment to begin sooner, while the brain is still significantly strengthening and pruning neural networks. A paradigm shift is taking place on this issue, too. For a long time, scientists believed that functional deficits in certain brain regions caused autism–complications in brain structure that no change in wiring among neural networks would fix. Now they think symptoms arise because of communications problems between brain regions–problems that rewiring could solve if babies received specific therapy.

"The neuronal networks apparently do not coordinate very well," explains Fritz Poustka, director of child and adolescent psychiatry at Goethe University in Frankfurt, Germany. Poustka says regions that get too little input from other parts of the brain do not develop well. This effect is well known among children who were neglected when they were young, some isolated from almost all human contact. A child who develops this way shares some similar consequences, such as poor use of language and difficulty in making social connections. "A quick diagnosis of autism would enable us to stimulate the networks very early in life by deliberately providing the right inputs," Poustka says. He cannot say if such interventions would cure the disorder, but he believes that intensive behavioral training could make the symptoms milder.

Although Poustka doubts that markers in the blood would permit early diagnosis, he favors attempts to try to define telltale traits as young as possible to maximize the success of treatment. In speech development, for example, the best results are achieved when deliberate exercises are instituted before the child's second birthday. By the time a boy or girl is three or four, deficits can still be reduced, but fundamental changes are no longer possible, because the critical period during which speech develops has passed by.

Behaviors Untangled

Whether or not Amaral's project leads to common blood tests, it could prove beneficial to behavioral approaches as well because it includes developmentally delayed children. The standardized checklists that doctors now use for diagnosis, such as the autism diagnostic observation schedule, are adequate only for children who are at least one and a half to two and a half years old. And then, usually only for the so-called high functionals–autistic children with IQs over 80. The tests are inconclusive for many of the other suspected individuals because children who are delayed in their intellectual development often score similarly to children who truly have autism. It is difficult to determine whether cognitive problems are being misdiagnosed as symptoms of autism, Poustka says. Delay, or a completely different disorder, can prompt what appear to be autismlike patterns.

A Canadian research team is trying to clarify this overlap. Led by Lonnie Zwaigenbaum, now at the University of Alberta in Edmonton, the group devised a 16-point observational checklist called the Autism Observation Scale for Infants and used it to evaluate 65 one-year-old children, all of whom had older siblings with autism and therefore had an above-average chance of developing the disorder themselves. The researchers also assessed another 23 babies with no familial ties to or signs of autism.

Zwaigenbaum's group reappraised the children when they were two, this time using traditional tests. They found that almost all the children who were diagnosed as autistic at age two had seven or more distinguishing traits when they were only one. "The predictive power of these markers is remarkable," Zwaigenbaum says.

Even among children just six months old, certain behavioral patterns forecast the onset of the disorder, notably a passive temperament and low physical activity levels. By their first birthdays, the children who later turned out to be autistic were easily irritated, had problems with visual tracking, tended to focus on a very few objects, failed to look around for a speaker who said their name, and barely interacted with others. They also tended to have certain obsessive motions, such as stroking surfaces, yet made very few gestures toward other people. And they understood less spoken language than their age-mates who were later identified as nonautistic.

As Amaral acknowledged about his first blood-profile exploration, Zwaigenbaum notes that further studies must include children who are at risk for other developmental disorders to help distinguish which symptoms are specific to autism. He is also open to the possibility of environmental influences in triggering or at least exacerbating autism. He says it is hard to know if the traits his group identified are early manifestations of the disorder or if they contribute to a pattern of development that may lead to autism.

Either way, his investigation, Amaral's and those of others are all improving our understanding of when autism starts, providing hope for earlier diagnosis and more effective treatment. The goal, of course, is to offer toddlers a greater chance at a more fruitful childhood, which in turn raises their chances for more satisfying years as teenagers and adults. The many challenges that autistic individuals face as they mature–learning, communicating with others, making and keeping friends, building life skills, securing a job, finding love—will be less daunting if they can get off to an earlier, better start.

Referenced

Behavioral Manifestations of Autism in the First Year of Life. Lonnie Zwaigenbaum et al. in *International Journal of Developmental Neuroscience*, Vol. 23, Nos. 23, pages 143152; AprilMay 2005.

Autistic Brains Out of Synch? Ingrid Wickelgren in *Science*, Vol. 308, pages 18561858; June 24, 2005.

About the Author

Ulrich Kraft is a contributor to Gehirn & Geist. *He wrote about disorders of the brain's timekeeping mechanism in the June/July 2007 issue of* Scientific American Mind.

Redefining Autism: Will New *DSM-5* Criteria for ASD Exclude Some People?

By Ferris Jabr

People have been arguing about autism for a long time—about what causes it, how to treat it and whether it qualifies as a mental disorder. The controversial idea that childhood vaccines trigger autism also persists, despite the fact that study after study has failed to find any evidence of such a link. Now, psychiatrists and members of the autistic community are embroiled in a more legitimate kerfuffle that centers on the definition of autism and how clinicians diagnose the disorder. The debate is not pointless semantics. In many cases, the type and number of symptoms clinicians look for when diagnosing autism determines how easy or difficult it is for autistic people to access medical, social and educational services.

The controversy remains front and center because the American Psychiatric Association (APA) has almost finished redefining autism, along with all other mental disorders, in an overhaul of a hefty tome dubbed the *Diagnostic and Statistical Manual of Mental Disorders (DSM)*—the essential reference guide that clinicians use when evaluating their patients. The newest edition of the manual, the *DSM-5*, is slated for publication in May 2013. Psychiatrists and parents have voiced concerns that the new definition of autism in the *DSM-5* will exclude many people from both a diagnosis and state services that depend on a diagnosis.

The devilish confusion is in the details. When the APA publishes the *DSM-5*, people who have already met the criteria for autism in the current *DSM-IV* will not suddenly lose their current diagnosis as some parents have feared, nor will they lose state services. But several studies recently published in child psychiatry journals suggest that it will be more difficult for new generations of high-functioning autistic people to receive a diagnosis because the *DSM-5* criteria are too strict. Together, the studies conclude that the major changes to the definition of autism in the *DSM-5* are well grounded in research and that the new criteria are more accurate than the current *DSM-IV* criteria. But in its efforts to make diagnosis more accurate, the APA may have raised the bar for autism a little too high, neglecting autistic people whose symptoms are not as severe as others. The studies also point out, however, that minor tweaks to the *DSM-5* criteria would make a big difference, bringing autistic people with milder symptoms or sets of symptoms that differ from classic autism back into the spectrum.

A New Chapter

Autism is a disorder in which a child's brain does not develop typically, and neurons form connections in unusual ways. The major features of autism are impaired social interaction and communication—such as delayed language development, avoiding eye-contact and difficulty making friends—as well as restricted and repetitive behavior, such as repeatedly making the same sound or intense fascination with a particular toy.

The *DSM-5* subsumes autistic disorder, Asperger's disorder, childhood disintegrative disorder, and pervasive developmental disorder not otherwise specified (PDD-NOS)—which are all distinct disorders in *DSM-IV*—into one category called autism spectrum disorder (ASD). The idea is that these conditions have such similar symptoms that they do not belong in separate categories, but instead fall on the same continuum.

Essentially, to qualify for a diagnosis of autistic disorder in *DSM-IV*, a patient must show at least six of 12 symptoms, which are divided into three groups: deficits in social interaction; deficits in communication; and repetitive and restricted behaviors and interests. In contrast, the *DSM-5* divides seven symptoms of ASD into two main groups: deficits in social communication and social interaction; and restricted, repetitive behaviors and interests.

The APA collapsed the social interaction and communication groups from *DSM-IV* into one group in the new edition because research in the last decade has shown that the symptoms in these groups almost always appear together. Research and clinical experience has also established that heightened or dulled sensitivity to sensory experiences is a core feature of autism, which is why it appears in *DSM-5* but not in the preceding version. The psychiatric community has generally applauded these changes to the criteria for ASD.

What is in question is how many of the *DSM-5* criteria a patient must meet to receive a diagnosis—too many and the manual excludes autistic people with fewer or milder symptoms; too few and it assigns autism to people who don't have it. Since the 1980s the prevalence of autism has dramatically increased worldwide, especially in the U.S. where the Centers for Disease Control and Prevention estimates that nine per 1,000 children have been diagnosed with ASD. Many psychiatrists agree that the increase is at least partially explained by loose criteria in *DSM-IV*.

"If the *DSM-IV* criteria are taken too literally, anybody in the world could qualify for Asperger's or PDD-NOS," says Catherine Lord, one of the members of the APA's *DSM-5* Development Neurodevelopmental Disorders Work Group. "The specificity is terrible. We need to make sure the criteria are not pulling in kids who do not have these disorders."

Relaxed Requirements

Three studies published between last summer and this month conclude that the *DSM-5* criteria for ASD are too strict, but that a few small changes would make them appropriately inclusive. One might think that the APA would conduct such research themselves, but studies that explicitly compare *DSM-IV* and *DSM-5* criteria are not an official part of the revision process. Rather, researchers who are not helping revamp the *DSM*, but were interested in how the new edition will change psychiatric diagnosis, decided to find out for themselves.

Marja-Leena Mattila of the University of Oulu in Finland conducted the only epidemiological study published so far that explicitly compared the two editions' criteria for autism. (Mattila used *DSM-5* criteria posted to the DSM-5 Development Web site in February 2010; the criteria have the same basic structure as the new specifications posted in January 2011, but they are far less detailed and descriptive.) In her study, Mattila surveyed a sample of more than 5,000 Finnish schoolchildren and identified 26 eight-year-olds with an IQ of 50 or higher who qualified for autistic disorder in the *DSM-IV*. Of those 26, only 12 qualified for ASD in the *DSM-5*. But when Mattila lowered the threshold for ASD by requiring only two of the three symptoms in the social interaction and communication group, 25 of the 26 children qualified for ASD in the both the *DSM-5* and its predecessor. Her work appears in the June 2011 issue of the *Journal of the American Academy of Child and Adolescent Psychiatry*.

Similarly, Thomas Frazier of the Center for Autism at the Cleveland Clinic performed a series of statistical analyses on symptom reports from nearly 7,000 ASD children, looking for the symptoms that appeared together most frequently. When he programmed a computer to figure out what kind of diagnostic model best reflected the naturally occurring clusters of symptoms, Frazier found that a model with two groups of symptoms—just like the one in the *DSM-5*—captured how the symptoms clustered in the children better than the *DSM-IV* or any other model. He also found that the *DSM-5* model misdiagnosed autism in only 3 percent of the children, whereas the *DSM-IV* model misdiagnosed autism in 14 percent. When Frazier relaxed the *DSM-5* requirements from five out of seven criteria to four out of seven, he brought back about 12 percent of ASD children that the model originally neglected.

William Mandy of University College London also used statistical analyses to evaluate the *DSM-5* criteria and concluded that the two-group *DSM-5* model is overall more accurate than the three-group *DSM-IV* model, but a little too restrictive. Both Frazier's study and Mandy's study are published this month in the *Journal of the American Academy of Child and Adolescent Psychiatry*.

"They got the major changes right," Mandy says of the APA. "But recent evidence shows that borderline people might miss out on a diagnosis in *DSM-5* because they don't have clinical levels of some symptoms, such as repetitive behavior. The real issue is threshold." Not all psychiatrists agree that the stricter *DSM-5* criteria should be relaxed, because they think that many people currently diagnosed with Asperger's or PDD-NOS do not in fact have autism and that the new definition of ASD should not include these people. Some parents of children with severe autism are also in favor of stricter criteria, arguing that children who are most in need should receive state services over others with milder symptoms.

Darrel Regier, vice chair of the *DSM-5* Task Force, says that he is well aware of the recent studies and that the committee will consider whether they need to revise the *DSM-5* criteria for ASD even further. The APA is supposed to finalize all changes to the *DSM* this year and publish the new edition in May 2013. When asked if he thinks the APA can adjust the revisions to criteria not only for ASD, but for all the other disorders in the *DSM-5* by the end of this year, Regier says "there is plenty of time."

About the Author

Ferris Jabr is a contributing writer for Scientific American. *He has also written for the* New York Times Magazine, *the* New Yorker *and* Outside.

Early Intervention Could Help Autistic Children Learn to Speak

By Marissa Fessenden

Autistic children struggle with many obstacles, including learning to speak. And, experts have noted, if these children learn verbal skills by age five, they tend to become happier and higher-functioning adults than do their nonverbal peers. Thirty years ago, psychiatrists expected only half of all autistic children would gain speaking abilities. Recent studies, however, indicate that as many as 80 percent of children with autism can learn to talk. One such study in 2006 showed that toddlers who received intensive therapy aimed at developing foundational oral language skills made significant gains in their ability to communicate verbally. Now researchers have followed up with a number of those kids and found that most of them continued to reap the benefits of that therapy years after it had ended.

Several early behaviors build a foundation for language. These abilities have also been linked to whether a child can anticipate another person's mental state and use that understanding to explain and predict behavior. Developing this "theory of mind" may be a central difficulty for children with autism. Kasari's team targeted two of the early behaviors in their work: The first is the ability to engage in symbolic play, in which one object represents another–a child pretending a doll is his parent, for instance. The second is joint attention, wherein a child divides focus between an object and another person. This behavior can be thought of as "sharing looks." For example, when a child points to show a playmate a toy train, she looks at the moving train and checks to see if her playmate is engaged.

In the initial study, Connie Kasari of the University of California, Los Angeles, and her colleagues evaluated 58 children between three and four years old in a randomized controlled study. The children played with trained graduate students for 30 minutes each day over a period of five to six weeks. The time-intensive interventions focused on either symbolic play or joint attention. A third group, serving as a control, participated in playtime but was not directed to complete tasks and goals.

Independent clinical testers assessed the children before and after the intervention. They measured language and cognitive skills with standard tests, evaluated play level and diversity, and interaction with a caregiver. The initial study, published in 2006, showed that the joint-attention group was better at showing and pointing behavior whereas the symbolic play group showed more symbolic behavior, both in terms of play level and diversity. Twelve months after the therapy period, Kasari's group assessed the kids' language skills. On a standard language test, the two intervention groups showed spoken language improvement that corresponded to 15 to 17 months of development; the control group had only made a nine-month gain during the same period. Younger children and children at the lowest language levels prior to the intervention made the largest improvements. Kasari was initially surprised the groups showed such progress. The most important aspect of both interventions, she says, was "engaging the child for periods of time with a social partner."

In the new study, Kasari's team revisited 40 of the children five years later. The researchers found that 80 percent of them, who were by then eight to nine years old, still had "useful, functional spoken language." A small number of children remained nonverbal, which Kasari says is typical for studies of children with autism. Some children do not seem to be able to learn useful language by age five, but studies suggest it is possible to acquire language later. The new studies show a method for teaching preschool-aged children basic skills that will help them develop language by five and continue to make improvements years later. The researchers detail their findings in the May issue of the *Journal of the American Academy of Child and Adolescent Psychiatry*.

Previous studies have targeted skills important to language development, but many only looked at small groups of children or infrequent treatment sessions, Kasari notes. Understanding what makes a treatment successful or not is vital. "We need to distill down the active ingredients in early intervention," she says, "then take these elements and match them to programs."

This kind of long-term follow-up is rare. "The study is important in terms of raising expectations of what can be accomplished, and in raising awareness of how much work it takes," says Sally J. Rogers, a psychiatry professor with the MIND Institute at the University of California, Davis. Rogers, who was not involved in the research, emphasized that because the subjects were very young, the study builds on evidence indicating that the earlier the intervention the better–and children even younger than the toddlers in the original study could benefit. This has important pubic policy implications, she says, because there is little funding for children younger than three.

Finding a one-size-fits-all approach to helping autistic kids talk may be tricky, however: Autism affects each child differently, Rogers observes, and even the best interventions will have varied outcomes.

About the Author

Marissa is a freelance science journalist in Bozeman, Montana. She was an editorial intern with Scientific American *from June 2012 through June 2013.*

On the Brink of Breakthroughs in Diagnosing and Treating Autism

By Geraldine Dawson

There's a popular saying in the autism community: "If you've met one person with autism, you've met one person with autism." Although this phrase is meant to convey the remarkable variation in abilities and disabilities among people with autism spectrum disorder (ASD), we're learning that it also applies to the extraordinary variability in how ASD develops. When I first began doing research on autism decades ago, we thought of it as one condition and aimed to discover its "cause." Now we know ASD is actually a group of lifelong conditions that can arise from a complex combination of multiple genetic and environmental factors. In the same way that each person with ASD has a unique personality and profile of talents and disabilities, each also has a distinct developmental history shaped by a specific combination of genetic and environmental factors.

More evidence of this extraordinary variety will be presented this week in Baltimore, where nearly 2,000 of the world's leading autism researchers will gather for the International Meeting for Autism Research (IMFAR). As president of the International Society for Autism Research, which sponsors the conference, I am more impressed than ever with the progress we are making. New findings being presented at the conference will highlight the importance of the prenatal period in understanding how various environmental factors such as exposure to alcohol, smoking and certain chemical compounds can increase risk for ASD. The impact of many environmental factors depends, however, on an individual's genetic background and the timing of the exposure. Other research links inflammation–detected in blood spot tests taken at birth–with a higher likelihood of an ASD diagnosis later on. Researchers suggest that certain factors such as maternal infection and other factors during pregnancy may influence an infant's immune system and contribute to risk. As our knowledge of these risk factors grows, so do the opportunities for promoting healthy pregnancies and better outcomes.

Autism in the Developing Brain

Among the most exciting developments in the field are results from a large-scale longitudinal study of the brains of infants with older siblings who have autism. About 20 percent of these infants will develop ASD. This study is providing an in-depth picture of how the brain develops in a child with autism and how this differs from a neurotypical child. State-of-the-art brain-imaging techniques are revealing the physical connections among different brain regions. By examining these detailed scans, researchers have detected differences in brain circuitry in infants who later develop ASD. Such differences are evident during the first year of postnatal life and can help us detect ASD as soon as—or even before—symptoms emerge. The goal is to start intervention even earlier in development when the brain is rapidly developing and most plastic. We have come a long way from the studies my colleagues and I conducted in the 1990s in which we used home videotapes to detect early symptoms of autism.

Research on brain development is helping us understand why people with autism have difficulty navigating the social world, and also why many show exceptional talents in areas such as math, music and art. Studies have found that long-range connections between different brain regions are weaker in people with ASD. Complex behaviors such as social interaction and language depend on the precise coordination of distant brain regions. Some studies have found that people with ASD have enhanced short-range neural connections, which might explain why ASD can be associated with exceptional skills in specific domains, such as visual memory. These brain differences also can lead to unusual perceptual and sensory experiences, including both heightened and reduced sensitivity to sound, sight, touch and other inputs. Several studies, for example, are exploring how people with autism perceive pain, especially those who engage in self-injury. Findings suggest that brain regions that typically respond when pain is felt are not as active.

We are also learning more about the role of gender in autism. When I first began working in the clinic, we would see five or six boys for every girl on the spectrum. Nearly all research was focused on boys. In recent years this has begun to change. We have come to realize that females with ASD often have different and milder symptom profiles than do boys, causing their diagnosis to be missed or delayed. This means girls are often missing out on access to early intervention—a fact that might explain why they often struggle more than boys do in areas such as daily living skills. In fact, research on females with ASD is leading us to question whether we need new or adapted screening or diagnostic tools to ensure that girls aren't put at a disadvantage.

Better Targeted Treatments

This year at IMFAR, a number of promising new treatments will be unveiled. Increasingly these are targeted to the individual. For example, many people with ASD also suffer from anxiety or attention deficits, and research shows that addressing these challenges can greatly improve their quality of life. The next frontier is to devise treatments for specific genetic subtypes. For example, people with a rare genetic syndrome called tuberous sclerosis complex (TSC) often develop autism. Researchers have identified a specific pathway in the brain—the mTOR signaling pathway—that is disrupted in people with TSC. By inhibiting this pathway in mice, they've managed to reverse ASD symptoms. Scientists are now working to translate this promising work to humans. Because TSC can be diagnosed before ASD symptoms are present, this work offers the hope of preventing cognitive impairment and other symptoms.

Whereas we are encouraged by the prospects for new treatments, we remain challenged in helping people access interventions that are already well established, such as early behavioral therapy. Cost and culture stand as barriers to many who would benefit. We also must do a better job of helping adults with ASD. Some of the research to be presented in Baltimore examines the effectiveness of adult interventions that range from cognitive training to mindfulness-based therapies. Studies are finding that treatments for autism must cover the whole life span and consider the broader context in which the person with autism lives, including family and community. We increasingly recognize the importance of providing support to the whole family, including siblings.

For much of the past two decades, popular discussion of autism has focused on the puzzling rise in its prevalence. That rise might have leveled off. According to the latest report from the Centers U.S. Centers for Disease Control and Prevention, the prevalence in children is holding steady at one in every 68 children. Now our attention must turn to ensuring that each unique person with ASD can reach his or her full potential and enjoy a meaningful and productive life. As a researcher and a clinician working every day with people with ASD and their families, I am more encouraged than ever about our progress in understanding a condition that was largely a mystery just two decades ago.

The views expressed are those of the author(s) and are not necessarily those of Scientific American.

About the Author

Geraldine Dawson is director of the Duke Center for Autism and Brain Development and a professor in the departments of Psychiatry and Behavioral Sciences, Pediatrics, and Psychology and Neuroscience at Duke University. She currently serves as president of the International Society for Autism Research and as a member of the National Institutes of Health Interagency Autism Coordinating Committee.

Autism Starts Months before Symptoms Appear, Study Shows

By Karen Weintraub

Parents often notice the first signs of autism in their children at around 12 to 18 months. Maybe a child isn't making eye contact, or won't smile when mom or dad walks in the door.

But a new study suggests there is evidence of autism in the brain even earlier—well before a child's first birthday—and that the signs can be seen on a magnetic resonance imaging (MRI) scan. "We're learning that there are biological changes that occur at [the time] or before the symptoms start to emerge," says Geraldine Dawson, a clinical psychologist and autism researcher at Duke University who was not involved in the new work. "It's the ability to detect autism at its very earliest stages that's going to allow us to intervene before the full syndrome is manifest."

For the study, published this week in *Nature*, researchers conducted MRI scans on 150 children three times: at six months old, one year and two years. Just over 100 of the children were at high risk because they had an older sibling diagnosed with autism. The faster growth rate of the surface areas of their brains correctly predicted eight times out of 10 which of the high-risk children would go on to be diagnosed with the condition.

Enlargement of the brain seemed to correlate with the arrival of symptoms, says Heather Hazlett, a psychologist at the University of North Carolina's Carolina Institute for Developmental Disabilities (CIDD), and the paper's lead author. Still, with only 100 at-risk children, the study is too small to be considered definitive—nor should doctors rush to use MRIs to diagnose autism, Hazlett says.

But if the study results are confirmed in future research, it could offer a new option for screening high-risk children before their symptoms become obvious—and possibly at a time when treatment will be most effective. The faster pattern of brain growth "is a potential biomarker that could be used to identify those infants who perhaps could benefit from early stimulation," Dawson says. "This could help those children have the best outcomes."

Autism spectrum disorders—so called because they present a wide range, or spectrum, of different social and communication challenges—are often characterized by behaviors that include rocking motions or obsessions. Parents often do not notice things that would point to an autism diagnosis until about 18 months, when typical children are expected to be talking and interacting socially. By showing the child's neurobiology changes before behavior does, the study may help parents better understand their child's experience, says biopsychologist Alycia Halladay, chief science officer at the Autism Science Foundation, a nonprofit that supports research but was not involved in the new work.

By showing scientists more about how brains develop prior to an autism diagnosis, the study may also offer insights into the genetic triggers of autism, says James McPartland, a psychologist at Yale University's Child Study Center who also did not take part in the research. "When we know more about neural pathways, we can think more about the genetic pathways," he says.

One thing the study could not show is whether there is anything different about the autism in families that have more than one child with the condition, compared with autism that seems to have no familial connection. One in every 68 children is diagnosed with autism; but among the younger siblings of a child on the spectrum, the rate is as high as one in five.

A number of studies are underway among these younger siblings of children on the spectrum, often called "baby sibs," who are more likely to develop autism. This group is easier to study than the general population because fewer test subjects are needed to find children who will go on to develop autism. But it is not clear if these "baby sibs" are somehow categorically different from others on the spectrum.

To find enough children to make their study useful, the research team followed more than 500 infants, scanning many of them in the middle of the night so they would be in a deep sleep. It took years to get enough valid data on 150 of them, and the families volunteered their time. "Often we don't keep in mind the degree of work it takes to do this kind of study," Dawson says.

Hazlett and senior author Joseph Piven, a colleague at the CIDD, say they began the research about a decade ago, after an earlier study suggested the brains of autistic children were already unusually large by the time they reached their second birthdays—and before autism's behavioral symptoms usually emerge.

Piven, a psychiatrist, says the mechanism is not precisely clear. But he speculates babies who go on to become autistic experience the world differently in the first year of life than kids who will not have autism do—and that this altered experience of the world may contribute to subsequent brain development in autism.

Dawson says because the brain is changing so much in the first year of life, it may be a critical window of development when behavioral interventions—such as teaching a child to pay attention to a parent's facial expressions—might have the biggest effect. Because it has not been clear until recently that autistic differences begin as early as pregnancy and infancy, there are no therapies to treat such young children. But such treatments are currently being tested. By giving researchers a potential tool to diagnose babies, Dawson says the new study could open up possibilities for testing the potential new therapies.

McPartland described possible treatments as "hyper-parenting." Whereas it might be okay to leave a neurotypical child to play with a toy, a child headed for autism might benefit from more interaction, he says, with a parent cooing, laughing and singing. "Supersaturate a child's environment with social information much as you can," he says. "And hope that it takes."

About the Author

Karen Weintraub is a staff writer at USA Today, *where she covers COVID, vaccine development and other health issues.*

Is It Time to Give Up on a Single Diagnostic Label for Autism?

By Simon Baron-Cohen

Five years ago, the American Psychiatric Association (APA) established autism spectrum disorder (ASD) as an umbrella term when it published the fifth edition of the *Diagnostic and Statistical Manual (DSM-5)*, the primary guide to taxonomy in psychiatry. In creating this single diagnostic category, the APA also removed the subgroup called Asperger syndrome that had been in place since 1994.

At the 2018 annual meeting of the International Society for Autism Research (INSAR), there will be plenty of discussion about diagnostic terminology: Despite the many advantages of a single diagnostic category, scientists will be discussing whether, to achieve greater scientific or clinical progress, we need subtypes.

The Advantages of a Single Diagnostic Label

The APA created a single diagnostic label of ASD to recognize the important concept of the spectrum, since the way autism is manifested is highly variable. All autistic individuals share core features, including social and communication difficulties, unusually narrow interests, a strong need for repetition and, often, sensory issues. Yet these core features vary enormously in how they are manifested, and in how disabling they are. This variability provides one meaning of the term spectrum, and the single diagnostic label ASD makes space for this considerable variability.

The term spectrum also refers to the heterogeneity in autism. There are huge disparities in many areas, such as language development or IQ, and in the presence or absence of co-occurring medical conditions and disabilities. This heterogeneity is also part of what is meant by a spectrum. And some autistic people also have very evident talents. This is another sense of the term spectrum, and the single diagnostic label makes room for this source of diversity, too.

There have been other benefits of the ASD label: It allows the clinician to describe the person without shoehorning them into a rigid subgroup. Its flexibility also allows for individuals who previously transitioned between different subgroups. And it reduced the risk that service providers might exclude a person because they didn't meet the eligibility criteria based on a rigid subtype. So, the consensus among clinicians is that the addition of the word "spectrum" was helpful and long overdue. Most clinicians therefore find it useful to have the flexibility of the very broad single diagnostic label.

Among proponents of a single diagnostic label, there is some debate about whether we should call it ASD (autism spectrum disorder) or ASC (autism spectrum conditions). This is because some people find the word "disorder" potentially stigmatizing, and argue that the word "condition" is equally effective in signaling a medical diagnosis. But leaving this point aside, many scientists are debating what got lost when subgroups were dropped.

The Downsides of a Single Diagnostic Label

One main reason given by the APA for deleting Asperger Syndrome (AS) was that diagnosis was unreliable. With hindsight, we can see that differentiating AS from classic autism was not the problem. The problem was differentiating AS from high-functioning autism (HFA), a term used by some to refer to autistic people with a history of language delay but with an IQ in the average or above-average range.

Most everybody now agrees that the terms high- versus low-functioning were stigmatizing and therefore should be avoided, but the clear contrast between AS and classic autism might have had value and perhaps should have been retained and likely could have been distinguished with high reliability. And for many, the term AS had even become part of their identity; it felt like more than just a diagnosis.

A widely held view is that medicine makes more progress by identifying subgroups, and AS versus classic autism were two very useful subgroups, because they are quite different in terms of likely levels of independence and educational and occupational attainment. Many parents, such as Alison Singer in her keynote speech in the 2017 INSAR annual meeting, also argued that by lumping AS and classic autism together, the breadth of autistic individuals is not adequately represented–that the single diagnostic category benefits neither subgroup.

For those who may think we should revert to two major subgroups, it is no longer clear that AS would be the right name for one of these, given recently published research about Hans Asperger colluding with the Nazi eugenics program during World War II. Those in the autism community who identify as having AS, and others, are actively discussing this difficult question.

But the main argument against a single diagnostic label is that the inclusion of subtypes will likely lead to greater scientific progress in understanding the precise causes of the heterogeneity, and greater translational progress in understanding what kinds of interventions and support are needed, and for whom.

A Moderate Proposal

One obvious way forward would be to do what other medical diagnoses (such as Diabetes) have done, and introduce a typology of subgroups, as in type 1 and type 2. So, it's not about either having a single diagnostic label or subgroups. One can have both. Under this approach, we could keep the single umbrella category called the autism spectrum and within this have type 1, type 2, etc.

This could maintain the *DSM-5*'s flexibility, so that a person could transition freely between subtypes as they change across their development. Type 1 could be mapped on to what was formerly known as AS, and type 2 on to what was formerly known as classic autism. Other subtypes will undoubtedly follow, such as the syndromic forms of autism that are due to rare genetic mutations, to become type 3 and so on.

Some may worry that this simply reintroduces the high- versus low-functioning distinction. Others will say it avoids the stigmatizing language while recognizing the value of marking the significant differences within the spectrum. Some may argue that this places too much reliance on IQ tests that frequently underestimate the intelligence of autistic people, who might be mistakenly subtyped as type 2 when they are really type 1.

But by allowing flexible transitioning, there may be ways to get around this concern. Clinicians will need to have a very flexible notion of intelligence, and not stick rigidly to any specific test, such as a verbal IQ test.

Interestingly, the *DSM-5* does already have the option to recognize subtypes, referred to as "specifiers," and invites clinicians to use these to capture co-occurring conditions. But there may be value in explicitly recognizing subgroups within the autism spectrum, while keeping the helpful concept of specifiers. An individual could have type 1 autism with ADHD, or type 2 autism with language impairment, for example.

There will be others who argue that we should only subtype on the basis of biology, not psychology, since in other medical conditions such as diabetes, subgrouping into type 1 and type 2, etc., is based on discovering different causal/mechanistic factors, which have different prognostic or therapeutic implications.

I can't wait to be at the INSAR 2018 annual meeting this year to listen to the arguments about whether we should subtype the autism spectrum, and if so what is the most useful way to do so. And to learn about the latest cutting edge scientific research that can be harnessed to improve the lives of autistic people and their families.

The views expressed are those of the author(s) and are not necessarily those of Scientific American.

About the Author

Simon Baron-Cohen is director of the Autism Research Center at the University of Cambridge, UK, and president of the International Society for Autism Research.

We Need Better Diagnostic Tests for Autism in Women

By Zhara Astra

"You don't look autistic."

This is what people say when I first tell them I'm on the spectrum. But I do look autistic. The problem is that people, especially medical professionals, don't know what to look for when it comes to identifying and diagnosing autism in women and girls.

I am a professor, a screenwriter, producer, mother and a woman who has autism. The challenges I have had in getting my diagnosis lead me to believe that we have to develop a more accurate standard autism test and better diagnostic criteria specifically for women and girls. This test and these criteria need to be co-created by autistic women and psychologists who understand how autism manifests differently in women and girls.

The current assessment is a prime example of gender bias in medicine and an example of how diagnostics are rife with gender and racial biases. The latest diagnostic criteria for autism were set forth in the 2013 *Diagnostic and Statistical Manual of Mental Disorders* (*DSM-5*). This version has extremely restrictive requirements for an autism diagnosis, such as showing deficits in nonverbal communication, displaying social issues, using repetitive speech, and difficulty maintaining relationships.

These diagnostic requirements are outdated and more specific to the white male experience of autism, and until recently, most psychological testing done to diagnose autism was developed using the experiences and symptoms of cisgender white males. The *DSM* doesn't distinguish between subtypes of autism, including Asperger's syndrome. This means when women and girls visit their doctors with symptoms that lead them to think they have autism, they don't fit the diagnostic criteria, leading to no diagnosis or an incorrect one.

Developing a more accurate diagnostic test is an issue of safety, as well as quality of life, for so many women silently struggling to understand why they might be different, including myself.

Growing up in the 1990s, I was different from other girls, but I certainly never considered I had autism. Sure, I operated on a different wavelength: I gravitated towards philosophy and books that dissected the meaning of life. I was extremely literal, and had a fascination with math and numbers, as is common in autism.

But, less commonly, I didn't like to be touched, I laughed at inappropriate times, ate the same foods every day, and was frequently overstimulated by smells, textures and sounds. We are starting to discover that these traits are more likely to occur in women and girls with autism.

I was undoubtedly different, but because my traits were more subtle than what we typically consider a person with autism to have, and because I had become accustomed to masking these quirks (girls with autism and ADHD are masterful at doing this), no one suspected I was on the spectrum.

It wasn't until 2020, when I was in my 30s and researching autism for my son, that I began to suspect I was on the spectrum. There began my troubles. It took me a year to find a psychologist who offered testing for adults, who had an understanding of women with autism, and who wouldn't charge me $5,000 or more for an assessment, since my insurance wouldn't cover the testing.

Most places I called were clueless when it came to diagnosing adult women. These psychologists had little experience diagnosing girls as well. After a year of searching for a competent, available and affordable psychologist, I finally found one and got a diagnosis of autism in 2021. I was told I had Asperger's syndrome, but that since the release of the *DSM-5*, the term had been swept into the general definition of "autism spectrum disorder."

Because of the narrow and gendered diagnostic criteria, we're instead often told by the doctors that we have a menstrual-related mood disorder or anxiety, as I was told, or we're slapped with some other grossly inaccurate label. All through history, women have been mislabeled as hysterical, when I think many were likely just neurodivergent and trying to fit into a neurotypical world.

Because of these false labels and the lack of testing, we have historically been overlooked, misdiagnosed or undiagnosed entirely. Many of us end up self-diagnosing later in life, after years of wondering why we feel so out of place in this world and in our own bodies.

Anxiety and depression are very common in neurodivergent women, especially those who remain undiagnosed. Women with autism are three to four times more likely to attempt suicide than neurotypical women. Comorbidities are very common in autistic women as well and can dramatically enhance the risk. Research indicates that women with autism and attention deficit hyperactivity disorder have an even higher chance of trying to commit suicide.

We may look like "the mom next door," but our inner world tells a different story: a change in plans, a high-pitched sound, a blast of pungent perfume, or a stray label in a sweater, and we're suddenly struggling to avoid a meltdown.

It's exhausting and if you don't have the privilege of understanding why you feel this way, then it can be maddening. Knowing you have autism (along with other comorbid neurodivergences) and that you're prone to anxiety, depression and burnout can help suffering women get access to the treatment and support they may need.

But better diagnostic criteria are just the beginning. We also need more programs, like group therapy and support groups for women who are diagnosed with autism in adulthood. Training teachers, doctors and psychologists on what to look for in girls and women and how to accommodate us should also become the new standard.

Understanding autism in girls is also a matter of safety, as these girls are three times more likely to be sexually abused. We tend to be more trusting and naïve, because we are often very direct and straightforward and expect other people to be the same. Recognizing ill intentions and ulterior motives in others can be difficult for us. This can make us more vulnerable and susceptible to abuse.

Every person deserves the opportunity to succeed and rise to their greatness, including women with autism. As more girls and women recognize they are neurodivergent, having accurate testing and the accommodations means we have a better chance to do our best.

About the Author

Zhara Astra is a screenwriter, producer and a professor at Arizona State University where she teaches a course she created on Understanding Neurodivergent Women.

Coming Out Autistic

By Brandy Schillace

I was late for lunch. At the time, I was juggling a teaching position with my work as public engagement fellow and running a journal; I'd made an appointment to meet a new graduate student assistant—but time got away from me. I was out of breath by the time I arrived, head still spinning with the effort of code-switching from one role to the next. It would take a few minutes to pull myself together, but the student was already there. I sat down, attempted some small talk (badly), rearranged my jacket on the chair four or five times. When I got myself in order, we commenced our discussion of the journal as we waited on sandwiches.

"I want to ask you something," she said. "How do you keep all your personas straight? I mean, how do you keep from losing yourself, being autistic and all?"

"I am not autistic," I corrected. She put down her lunch.

"But you are. Just like me."

She meant no offense. But I felt outed, vulnerable. I'd worked most of my life to present as "normal" and even believed it myself on good days. I couldn't accept her casual diagnosis. It would take a coming-out journey (my second) to help me arrive at a place of acceptance.

I do not (yet) have an official diagnosis for autism. This is by design. I was born in the late 1970s in the midst of a family crisis. My mother rescued us both from my biological father and keep me hidden away at my grandparents' house for fear he might violate her restraining order. I developed unusual behaviors. I could walk and talk in full sentences by the age of eight months. As a toddler I put thought bubbles above my crayon drawings with pictographs for meaning. I loved words. I memorized stories, poems, songs. My grandmother considered me "gifted." But in addition to these traits, I could scarcely be handled or touched. I could not be taken into enclosed or noisy spaces; I bit and scratched other toddlers.

I understand now that I suffer easily from sensory overload—I can get physically ill simply walking into a junk shop. Back then, I was just "being weird," and it was thought best if we kept it to ourselves.

In school, I had to adapt. It was hard going. I excelled in every subject and failed miserably (and embarrassingly) at social cues. But to my young mind, that was just part of growing up, and I wasn't as good at it as other people. Don't be weird, I told myself. Don't be weird.

I'm weird. I memorize lists of normative behaviors (introduce yourself, make eye contact, ask about the family, don't make those weird noises, don't tic in front of people, wear the right face for the job), but I never quite get it all right. Even so, I still did not think I was autistic. Being told I must be, by someone who was also autistic, distressed and shocked me. All of my associations for neurodivergence came with baggage.

I may never forgive *Rain Man*. Dustin Hoffman's portrayal of Raymond, the autistic elder brother of Charlie Babbitt (Tom Cruise) shows him unable to communicate effectively, prone to public meltdowns, and—because the doctor deems him "unable to make his own decisions" or function in society—ultimately in need of institutionalization. The film never provides Raymond's point of view—only the perspectives of those around him, who are entrusted to make his decisions for him. I was horrified by the movie. It frightened me. I understood very clearly that there were accepted norms, and that you could be locked away for violating them.

I knew I wasn't like other people. But I had also internalized the idea that this was "fixable," that I was curable. Adaptive behavior is recommended to parents of autistic kids today: help your child fit in socially, they say, as though autism were something to be schooled out of you by proper training. Masking may be a means of hiding who you are to prevent being outed (or harassed), but it comes with consequences, including anxiety, exhaustion—and loss of identity. And that, at least in part, was the question put to me by the graduate student when I arrived late to lunch: How do I present all these faces without losing my authenticity? It frightened me that I didn't have an answer.

In my early attempts to adapt, I used other human beings as look-books. I copied expressions, ways of being in the world, how to perform emotion so I could be better understood. I learned to see social interactions as a play; I can handle any genre—so long as I have the script and know the dress code. Trouble happens when there is no script, or someone changes it halfway through. I spent harrowing lunch hours driving home in traffic because I'd worn the wrong self for the day's activities. I can feel physically sick if I misread the type of attire expected for an occasion. It has been mistaken in me for vanity, but I'm not dressing to impress others so much as putting on the part required. It came natural to me to play both male and female parts; I excelled in almost any costume. I didn't know who I was without them.

I left my job in 2018. It should have been liberating; I'd just embarked on a freelance career and had a book contract. Working from home meant nothing to dress for, and without a specific role, I felt anxious and adrift. Similar experiences played out for people around the world in 2020 with pandemic lockdowns; I was an early adopter. I flipped from my work wardrobe of power suit-skirts and heels to men's jeans and T-shirts—but I felt between selves. Maybe there was a reason for that, my therapist suggested. Did I feel like a different gender from the one I was assigned? It wasn't a solution, but it was at least the right kind of question.

My body has always been a vehicle for the transportation and translation of ideas, and all the scattered performances were what I collectively called "myself." The specific bits of my body didn't really enter into the equation all that much. Many trans people experience terrible dysphoria over aspects of their bodies and seek to change them; some experience none and some fall between. For me, my gender felt wholly outside of, rather than a reflection of, myself. Extrinsic. I had mainly constructed it from other external cues.

I am married to a cisgendered and heterosexual (cis/het) man, and so most people assume I am a cis/het woman. I had neither expressed nor denied it; I just hadn't considered the question. I have always had traits largely considered "masculine," and my sexuality is pretty fluid, too. Mark intrigued and interested me; I fell in love with him for that, not because he was a man. So, I had to ask myself: was I just performing as cis/het?

For me, gender was something to be worn and used, a means of interacting with the world; I didn't know how to see it as an identity in and of itself. Jude Ellison S. Doyle wrote recently in an article titled "Divergent: The Emerging Research on the Connection between Trans Identities and Neurodivergence": "It wasn't possible to transition as long as I thought of myself as defective.... It was all so exhausting I could barely leave the house." I identified with that sentiment. I had been trying to choose a single new gender (and to do it right), but was still only expressing a part of who I am. In my search to understand what my identity meant to me, rather than how I packaged it for other people, I realized I am gender-fluid: nonbinary but containing multitudes. In that new freedom, I found myself returning to that other possibility. I had come out as gender fluid; could I also come out as autistic?

In August of 2020, the authors of the largest study to date on the overlap of autism and gender diversity announced their findings: about 25 percent of gender-diverse people have autism (compared to about 5 percent of cisgender people), leading them to suggest transgender and gender-diverse adults were between three and six times more likely to be diagnosed as autistic. As Doyle puts it, "'Autistic' is one of the most trans things you can be." So why isn't this connection more well-known?

One point, remarked on by Doyle and also by Eric Garcia in his new book *We're Not Broken: Changing the Autism Conversation*, is that autism is underdiagnosed along gendered lines. Cisgender men are identified as autistic more frequently, and at a much younger age, than either cisgender women or gender-diverse people. Even the autistic stereotypes are masculinized; an "extreme male brain" theory posits that autistic people process the world through a "male" lens. In truth, there are no significant differences between male and female brains—but, as Garcia points out, some autistic behaviors are seen as "female behaviors." It is more likely, then, that a boy who behaves neuro-atypically will be recognized and diagnosed. If parents, teachers and therapists are seeing symptoms along a binary of gender, they're going to miss people, and among gender-nonconformists, it's a significant percentage.

For many, an acceptance of autism diagnosis leads to a questioning of gender normative rules and an embrace of gender diversity. Garcia quotes Charlie Garcia-Spiegel, a presenter at Autspace, a conference on, for, and by neurodivergent people: "We [autistic people] can see a lot of the social rules around gender are bullshit, basically." It suggests that the 25 percent of autistics identifying as trans have been freed to do so by their autism. For me, this occurred in reverse. Questioning how I felt about my gender(s) gave me license to look at the other performed behaviors I'd learned to cultivate. It's also made me realize how much I have been impacted by social expectations, and how hard I had worked to meet them over the years.

As Eryn Star, an autistic and transmasculine writer and advocate emphasizes, trans people encounter prejudice, violence and denial of access to health care and other services. Some people claim they are illegitimate and want to prohibit them from living authentic lives. At the same time, people with autism are frequently rendered as incapable of making decisions for themselves about their sexuality. This increasingly public disdain and discrimination against trans and autistic people has surprising champions, including author J. K. Rowling, who suggested that autistic trans people assigned female at birth (AFAB) were being pressured to transition. (The autistic community responded with the hashtag #WeAreNotConfused.) "I have faced," says Star, "the denial of my queerness because I am disabled." Living authentically as both trans and neuro-atypical means confronting what I had always feared: if you cannot ape normativity, you may be denied your autonomy.

For years, I feared acknowledging my autism because I had absorbed the prejudice surrounding disability. Autistic people (as Garcia's book title emphasizes) are not broken. Autism is disabling because we live in a world built for and by neurotypical people. Acknowledging my autism is not an admission of weakness; it's a statement about myself as a self.

For Star, rediscovering their body as an autistic person no longer repressed by social pressure led to discoveries about their gender as transmasculine nonbinary. For comedian Hannah Gadsby, the late diagnosis of autism led her to "be kinder to myself" and "not always to take the responsibility." Both early and late diagnosis with autism offers a window into understanding our own identities. I've learned that I have a right to ask for and expect accommodation. Neurotypicals think they are meeting us halfway because they don't realize we've already come miles and miles just to get here. I am neurodivergent. I can be forgiven for missing cues and instead be honored for how much work goes into social interactions, all the time.

So much of this—perhaps all of this—comes down to acceptance, accommodation and justice. After a lifetime of trying to perfect myself, I'm finally living in my own authenticity: autistic, genderfluid, unique. I'm still in the play. But if I don't have a script, I can write my own, or I can cut the scene and draw the curtain. No matter how we identify, trans, neurodivergent, neuroqueer, we have a right to be—just as we are.

About the Author

Brandy Schillace is editor in chief of BMJ's Medical Humanities *journal and author of the recently released book* Mr. Humble and Doctor Butcher, *a biography of Robert White, who aimed to transplant the human soul.*

Section 3: What Causes Autism Spectrum Disorder?

What Really Causes Autism

By Simon Makin

Seven actors stand around a circle of swirling colors—blue, gold and white painted in the middle of the stage. Interspersed among them are twice as many children. Most of the younger players look withdrawn. Many appear disabled, intellectually or physically. One girl, about 12 years old, sits quietly in an electric wheelchair. The professional cast take turns, enticing their young charges into the center of the colorful "island," where they play simple games—practicing facial expressions and chanting words—all based on emotional scenes from Shakespeare's play *The Tempest*.

Every child engages, even those who initially seem unreachable. Many react with unquestionable joy. It is possibly one of the most moving things I've ever witnessed. But this experience isn't really for the audience. My ticket reads: "*The Tempest*, Suitable for 8–24-year-olds with autism," and the production showcases a novel therapy for autism spectrum disorder (ASD). The approach—pioneered by Kelly Hunter of the Royal Shakespeare Company and developed in conjunction with psychologists at Ohio State University—is unproved. But the idea behind it is compelling: core abilities involved in drama match up strikingly well with what is often described as the main triad of impairments in ASD: problems with social interaction, communication and imagination. In short, the actors are gifted in the very things that are deficient in the young participants and able to reach powerfully across the divide of disability.

The diversity of the children onstage is a telling reflection of just how complicated autism is behind the scenes. An official diagnosis calls for the trio of difficulties described above, along with repetitive behaviors—typically hand flapping, rocking or head banging—before the age of three. That said, ASD sufferers exhibit a wide range of both physical and neurological symptoms. High-functioning people with autism, including those with Asperger's syndrome (a diagnosis that was recently cut from the American Psychiatric Association's manual of disorders), have normal and sometimes high IQs and often show only mild to moderate social deficits. At the other end of the spectrum, children with profound autism are often intellectually disabled and so socially detached that they seem locked in a world of their own.

Complicating the clinical picture, the condition often coincides with other diagnoses, such as anxiety disorders, attention-deficit/hyperactivity disorder (ADHD), depression and epilepsy. According to the latest estimates, ASD affects one in 68 children. For decades researchers have debated its cause—an argument that grew increasingly urgent in the past 25 years as diagnostic rates soared. But recent studies have pretty well settled the question: autism is primarily genetic in origin, although it does not follow a simple hereditary pattern. Thanks to advances in DNA sequencing and collaborative efforts to pool data sets from laboratories around the world, scientists have found scores of genes that appear to be strongly linked to the disorder and many more that may also play supporting roles.

These new discoveries are offering important clues about the biology underlying ASD, insights that could eventually lead to targeted drug therapy. There is also a dawning realization that neurodevelopmental disorders in general—from autism to Down syndrome—may result not just from abnormal brain development but also from ongoing dysfunctional processes. The promise in that revelation is tremendous: although early interventions will remain vital in helping afflicted children reach their greatest potential, the hope is that even in adults, some aspects of ASD may one day be treatable.

Searching for the Cause

There is a saying common among people familiar with autism: "If you've met *one* person with autism, you've met one person with autism." This diversity is also proving true of the genetics behind the disorder. About one in 10 cases can be traced to mutations affecting a single gene. These so-called monogenic varieties generally occur as part of multifaceted syndromes that also cause physical malformations: fragile X, Phelan-McDermid, Rett and Timothy syndromes, as well as tuberous sclerosis and neurofibromatosis, to name a few.

Far more often ASD is considered idiopathic, meaning its root cause is unknown. Twin studies from as far back as the 1970s indicated that ASD was strongly heritable, but the subsequent rise in diagnoses led many researchers and parents to look for environmental influences. Currently experts believe that much of the increase stems from growing awareness among parents, pediatricians and educators and improved diagnostic criteria. Psychiatrist Terry Brugha of the University of Leicester in England and his colleagues found evidence in support of this idea in 2011, showing that a representative sample of previously undiagnosed adults had rates of ASD that were similar to recent estimates for children.

In recent years the evidence for genetic causes has advanced dramatically. A barrage of studies has produced a steady stream of genes strongly linked to autism. Some estimate that the number of associated genes may ultimately top 1,000. One especially important discovery is the role that so-called de novo mutations play. These glitches in the genetic code occur spontaneously in a sperm or egg cell and so are not inherited from either parent.

In 2007 molecular biologist Michael Wigler of Cold Spring Harbor Laboratory, geneticist Jonathan Sebat, now at the University of California, San Diego, and their colleagues noted some of the first de novo mutations linked to ASD in the form of copy-number variants—alterations in chromosomes that involve the deletion or duplication of whole chunks of DNA, which can affect multiple genes. Soon other scientists started to find autism-linked de novo point mutations (also referred to as single-nucleotide variants because they are one-letter changes in the DNA) implicating specific genes. Since then, a rash of studies has homed in on several de novo mutations (both copy-number variations and single-nucleotide variants) that substantially raise an individual's risk for ASD—sometimes 20-fold and, in rare cases, even 80-fold.

At the same time, multiple studies found that de novo mutations increase with paternal age. For instance, in 2012 Brian O'Roak, then working in geneticist Evan Eichler's lab at the University of Washington, and his colleagues discovered that 80 percent of spontaneous point mutations occur within sperm cells and that the number of mutations tends to increase with a father's age. The findings explain a small percentage of the known increase in risk for autism among children of older fathers.

Last November two studies published simultaneously in *Nature* upped the total number of genes linked to autism from around nine to more than 70. Both investigations used a technique called whole exome sequencing, which focuses exclusively on exons, regions of the genome containing code for building proteins. This approach lets researchers quickly and more affordably screen the 1 percent of the human genome we know the most about.

The first report, by Wigler, Eichler, Matthew State of the University of California, San Francisco, and their colleagues, analyzed the exomes of more than 2,500 families from the Simons Simplex Collection, a set of DNA samples from so-called simplex families who, by definition, have only one child with autism. By comparing each child's genome with their parents', the researchers estimated that de novo mutations contributed to around 30 percent of ASD diagnoses in these families and to 45 percent of diagnoses in girls. They also identified 27 genes strongly linked to ASD.

The second study came from the Autism Sequencing Consortium (ASC), involving researchers from 37 different institutions, by neuroscientist Joseph D. Buxbaum of the Icahn School of Medicine at Mount Sinai and his colleagues. Buxbaum—together with State, geneticist Mark Daly of the Broad Institute in Cambridge, Mass., and statisticians Kathryn Roeder of Carnegie Mellon University and Bernie Devlin of the University of Pittsburgh—founded the consortium in 2010, with support from the National Institute of Mental Health, to share samples and data. Looking for both inherited and spontaneous mutations, the team analyzed 3,871 autism cases and 9,937 unaffected individuals. They identified 33 genes strongly linked to ASD and more than 70 additional candidates. The genes implicated in these two studies overlap somewhat. Roeder reports that, along with geneticist Stephan Sanders of U.C.S.F., she has produced an unpublished list that includes genes affected by de novo copy variants. The top 71 of these genes are 90 percent likely to be involved in autism.

Adding Up the Risks

Most of the genes identified in the second study fall into three main categories. Some are involved in synaptic function—or how nerve cells in the brain communicate across the gaps, or synapses, between them. Some contribute to transcription, the process by which DNA is translated into proteins. And some play a role in remodeling chromatin—densely packed complexes of DNA and proteins whose changing structure determines which stretches of DNA are accessible for transcription. Because the latter two actually influence the activity of genes, they, too, may ultimately affect the growth and function of neurons and synapses.

These are mission-critical processes within and between cells, and so any disruptions during development could have far-reaching biological consequences. As such, these findings may explain evidence suggesting that ASD shares much of its genetic origins with other conditions, especially other developmental psychiatric disorders, such as schizophrenia, but also seemingly unrelated ones, such as congenital heart disorders. Researchers think that whether these genes actually trigger autism or something else or nothing at all may depend on the rest of a person's genetic makeup.

For instance, a specific high-risk mutation might potentially lead to a range of diseases or disabilities but will cause autism in those families whose inherited "genetic background" increases that particular risk. "There are some factors—not many—that increase risk enormously, some that increase it *a lot*, some that increase it some and a lot that increase risk a tiny bit," Buxbaum explains. "The manifestation of autism is the sum of all that risk in each individual, with some liability threshold, which differs for boys and girls."

More than four times as many boys are diagnosed with ASD as are girls. No one is exactly sure why, beyond assuming that girls are somehow protected from the effects of some mutations. A 2014 study by Sébastien Jacquemont, then at the University of Lausanne in Switzerland, and his colleagues found support for this idea, showing that affected girls tend to have more severe mutations. Also, these mutations were much more likely to have been inherited from the girls' mothers. One implication is that mothers can pass ASD-linked mutations on to their children without having the disorder themselves. These findings, together with the newly found importance of de novo mutations, may help explain why so many cases appear in families with no previous autism diagnoses.

De novo mutations seem to tip the balance in only about 14 percent of cases. Such severe mutations are rare precisely because they have a big effect and so reduce the likelihood of their carriers having children. "The usual reason a variant is rare is that it's brand-new in the population," Roeder says. Still, they offer a promising research avenue in that damaging genetic rarities often reveal more about the biological mechanisms of a disease than common, less harmful variants can. "We've learned a tremendous amount about cancer, hyperlipidemia, neurodegenerative disorders, and more through rare variations that account for a fleetingly small proportion of the population risk but have opened up compelling and widely applicable insights into biology," State observes. (For example, it was a gene for a rare, familial form of Parkinson's disease that led scientists to appreciate the role of the protein alpha-synuclein in all forms of the disorder.)

To date, researchers have had less luck nailing down the common genetic variations linked to ASD. Common variants collectively account for more of the risk of autism than rare ones do, but they individually confer such small increases that they are hard to identify. "At this point we have not pinpointed what specific common variants are relevant," says geneticist Benjamin Neale of the Broad Institute, who worked on the ASC study. "But there are multiple reports that common variation has a substantial influence."

The interplay among different kinds of variation–rare, common, inherited and spontaneous–is key to understanding the genetics of autism, scientists say. This past February geneticist Stephen Scherer of the University of Toronto and his colleagues published the results of a study in which they sequenced the entire genomes of 85 so-called quartet families–two parents and two ASD siblings. It turned out that nearly 70 percent of these affected brothers and sisters had *different* rare variants previously linked with autism. Buxbaum speculates that these families may have different underlying risks because of common variation, which when combined with rarer, possibly spontaneous, variants push individual children over the ASD threshold. "I think that's what's going on," he says. "The family has increased risk, and then the two siblings have different final causes."

To try to parse the relative contributions of common and rare variations, Roeder and Devlin have developed statistical tools to extend the methods for estimating the heritability of a trait. Together with Buxbaum and his colleagues in the Population-Based Autism Genetics and Environment Study Consortium (PAGES), they evaluated more than 3,000 people from Sweden's universal health registry, including more than 450 with ASD. After their analysis, they estimated that 49 percent of the total risk for ASD stems from common variants, whereas only 6 percent is from rare mutations (3 percent inherited, 3 percent de novo). Other studies have shown that another 4 percent can be credited to things such as recessive genes. But that still leaves 41 percent unexplained.

From Genes to Biology

Some of this missing risk could reflect environmental factors–perhaps infections, or certain drugs or toxins in the mother's system during pregnancy, or birth complications–any of which might permanently alter the expression of genes (a gene-environment interaction known as epigenetics) or increase risk in other ways. But additional phenomena are involved, from random chance to somatic mutations, which are not present in the egg or sperm but arise in cells as they divide during development. In rare cases, autism has been associated with mutations in mitochondrial DNA, inherited exclusively through the maternal line. And the gut microbiome might be implicated. Some people with autism appear to harbor unusual communities of bacteria in the digestive tract that can produce waste that harms the brain.

Moreover, ASD genes do not act in isolation but interact with one another, the environment and other biological processes in complex ways we are only beginning to understand. All these additional factors help to explain why identical twins—who have nearly exactly the same DNA—are only somewhere between 80 to 90 percent likely to share an ASD diagnosis. (When they do not both have autism, the twin without it will often have another psychiatric diagnosis, such as ADHD.)

To find out where, and *when*, in the brain genes linked to autism interact and begin to cause problems, scientists are turning to cutting-edge projects such as the BrainSpan Atlas of the Developing Human Brain, developed by the Allen Institute for Brain Science in Seattle in collaboration with several universities. This dynamic atlas charts the activation of genes in the brain throughout development, from a fetus to an adult. Several recent studies have combined these data with genetic findings. In doing so, researchers can map networks of genes that are expressed together in specific brain regions and cell types at the same time.

These investigations have revealed that many ASD-linked genes appear to function together in parts of the cortex during the mid- to late-fetal period, roughly five months after conception. Some studies specifically implicate what are known as projection neurons—cells responsible for forging long-range connections from one part of the brain to another. The finding bolsters some prominent theories that trace autism symptoms to abnormalities in how the brain is wired. Among those theories: there is an excess of local connections and insufficient long-distance ones.

Other scientists have considered not only where and when ASD genes are active in the brain but also how the proteins they produce interact. For instance, this past February systems biologist Lilia Iakoucheva of U.C.S.D. and her colleagues published findings from their investigation of an autism-linked copy-number variation known as 16p11.2. This stretch of chromosome 16 includes 29 different genes. Deletions increase the risk for autism; duplications increase the risk for both autism and schizophrenia.

Focusing on the genes found in this region, the team built up a related network of protein interactions. The researchers found that the protein produced by one 16p11.2 gene–called *KCTD13*–forms a structure with another protein, Cul3, during mid-fetal development. The *Cul3* gene lies in a different part of the genome but has been previously linked to autism in the form of de novo point mutations. Together these proteins control the levels of a third protein, RhoA, which is involved in choreographing the migration of cells in a developing brain.

The findings fit strikingly well with what was already known about how this mutation affects head size. When 16p11.2 regions are deleted, head size increases, whereas duplications decrease head size. (Larger than average head size is common among individuals with autism.) Iakoucheva says they were surprised to then find that mutations in a completely different gene, *CACNA1C*, which causes the rare form of autism called Timothy syndrome, have also been tied to this same RhoA mechanism. This convergence of three different mutations on the same biological process–one that might disrupt cell migration during fetal brain development–typifies much current thinking in the field: namely the suspicion that many of the 1,000 or more mutations that may be involved will ultimately converge on a limited number of underlying mechanisms.

The Path Ahead

Understanding exactly how ASD arises can only ease the anguish many parents have felt as they struggle to understand why the lightning bolt of severe autism happened to strike their family and worry that it will strike again. Scientists now have a set of genes they know will put a developing child at high risk for ASD, a list that can only grow. These findings will eventually transform diagnosis and facilitate earlier interventions. As genetic testing for autism expands and improves, parents with one affected child will be able to determine the risks that subsequent children may face. If the dominant cause of ASD in a firstborn is a de novo mutation, it might suggest little or no increased risk. Inherited mutations, on the other hand, could up the odds to something as high as 50 percent. Prenatal testing may also eventually become available.

Ultimately the goal is to develop effective treatments. One reason the American Psychiatric Association replaced Asperger's syndrome and other subtypes with the generic term "autism spectrum disorder" is that biological evidence for the old subtypes was lacking. But as genetic findings help researchers to uncover the biological mechanisms involved, it may lead to more individualized approaches to treatment, as is already happening in other areas of medicine. It may be that one day the diversity of the kids I watched participate in *The Tempest* will be matched by a similarly diverse array of therapeutic options.

"Gene discovery is the thing we're trying to get done as quickly as possible before we get down to the real work of understanding the biology and pathogenesis of the disorder and where we can usefully intervene," Buxbaum says. The mechanism identified by Iakoucheva and her colleagues, for example, offers one possible treatment target. She and her collaborators plan to use stem cell technology to investigate whether an existing drug called Rhosin, which alters RhoA protein levels in nerve cells, might be helpful. If it works, researchers will still face the challenge of how to deliver the drug to fetal brains because Rhosin cannot cross the blood-brain barrier.

Researchers have also made great strides in understanding the molecular biology of monogenic syndromes such as fragile X and Rett syndromes and have developed interventions that show promise in animal models of these conditions, which were previously thought to be completely irreversible. "Finding out that, at least in animal models, you can erase many of the consequences, even in adulthood, is tremendously exciting," State says.

The discoveries have led to preliminary drug trials. Buxbaum and his colleagues recently published preliminary findings from an early-stage clinical trial of insulinlike growth factor-1 (IGF-1) in nine children with Phelan-McDermid syndrome, which is caused by mutations in *SHANK3*, one of the highest-risk ASD genes. In all the children, who ranged in age from five to 15, the growth factor—which enhances the maturity of synapses—improved social functioning and lessened repetitive behaviors, such as rocking.

Additional studies show that IGF-1 may also help children with Rett syndrome, but whether it will benefit more genetically complex forms of ASD remains an open question. Buxbaum cautions that these preliminary results need to be replicated in larger samples, but it is worth noting that IGF-1 crosses the blood-brain barrier. Other researchers are testing substances found to reverse deficits in fragile X syndrome and tuberous sclerosis to see if they might work in genetically complex cases.

At the moment there are many ways forward for autism researchers. Larger samples and better study designs will enable new variants with smaller effects to be found, and whole genome sequencing will make it possible for scientists to identify risky mutations in the large parts of the genome they have not yet fully explored. As the resolution of BrainSpan and similar resources improves, they may reveal more about how these genes shape the developing brain. Over the long term, this will lead to new interventions for a condition for which effective treatment has been elusive. "That's really what we're trying to do," Buxbaum says. "Everything else is just steps toward that goal."

Referenced

Most Genetic Risk for Autism Resides with Common Variation. Trent Gaugler et al. in *Nature Genetics*, Vol. 46, No. 8, pages 881–885; August 2014.

The Contribution of De Novo Coding Mutations to Autism Spectrum Disorder. Ivan Iossifov et al. in *Nature*, Vol. 515, pages 216–221; November 13, 2014.

Synaptic, Transcriptional and Chromatin Genes Disrupted in Autism. Silvia De Rubeis et al. in *Nature*, Vol. 515, pages 209–215; November 13, 2014.

Autism Spectrum Disorders: From Genes to Neurobiology. A. Jeremy Willsey and Matthew W. State in *Current Opinion in Neurobiology*, Vol. 30, pages 92–99; February 2015.

Spatiotemporal 16p11.2 Protein Network Implicates Cortical Late Mid-Fetal Brain Development and KCTD13-Cul3-RhoA Pathway in Psychiatric Diseases. Guan Ning Lin et al. in *Neuron*, Vol. 85, No. 4, pages 742–754; February 18, 2015.

About the Author

Simon Makin is a freelance science journalist based in the UK. His work has appeared in New Scientist, The Economist, Scientific American, *and* Nature, *among others. He covers the life sciences, and specializes in neuroscience, psychology and mental health.*

The Concept of Neurodiversity Is Dividing the Autism Community

By Simon Baron-Cohen

At the annual meeting of the International Society for Autism Research (INSAR) in Montreal, Canada in May, one topic widely debated was the concept of neurodiversity. It is dividing the autism community, but it doesn't have to.

The term "neurodiversity" gained popular currency in recent years but was first used by Judy Singer, an Australian social scientist, herself autistic, and first appeared in print in the *Atlantic* in 1998.

Neurodiversity is related to the more familiar concept of biodiversity, and both are respectful ways of thinking about our planet and our communities. The notion of neurodiversity is very compatible with the civil rights plea for minorities to be accorded dignity and acceptance, and not to be pathologized. And while the neurodiversity movement acknowledges that parents or autistic people may choose to try different interventions for specific symptoms that may be causing suffering, it challenges the default assumption that autism itself is a disease or disorder that needs to be eradicated, prevented, treated or cured.

Many autistic people—especially those who have intact language and no learning difficulties such that they can self-advocate—have adopted the neurodiversity framework, coining the term "neurotypical" to describe the majority brain and seeing autism as an example of diversity in the set of all possible diverse brains, none of which is "normal" and all of which are simply different.

They argue that in highly social and unpredictable environments some of their differences may manifest as disabilities, while in more autism-friendly environments the disabilities can be minimized, allowing other differences to blossom as talents. The neurodiversity perspective reminds us that disability and even disorder may be about the person-environment fit. To quote an autistic person: "We are freshwater fish in salt water. Put us in fresh water and we function just fine. Put us in salt water and we struggle to survive."

There are also those who, while embracing some aspects of the concept of neurodiversity as applied to autism, argue that the severe challenges faced by many autistic people fit better within a more classical medical model. Many of these are parents of autistic children or autistic individuals who struggle substantially in any environment, who may have almost no language, exhibit severe learning difficulties, suffer gastrointestinal pain or epilepsy, appear to be in anguish for no apparent reason or lash out against themselves or others.

Many of those who adopt the medical model of autism call for prevention and cure of the serious impairments that can be associated with autism. In contrast, those who support neurodiversity see such language as a threat to autistic people's existence, no different than eugenics.

No wonder this concept is causing such divisions. Yet, I argue that these viewpoints are not mutually exclusive, and that we can integrate both by acknowledging that autism contains huge heterogeneity.

Before we address heterogeneity, a technical aside about terminology: The term "disorder" is used when an individual shows symptoms that are causing dysfunction and where the cause is unknown, while the term "disease" is used when a disorder can be ascribed to a specific causal mechanism. The term "disability" is used when an individual is below average on a standardized measure of functioning and when this causes suffering in a particular environment. In contrast, the term "difference" simply refers to variation in a trait, like having blue or brown eyes.

So what is the huge heterogeneity in the autism spectrum? One source of this is in language and intelligence: As I hinted at, some autistic people have no functional language and severe developmental delay (both of which I would view as disorders), others have milder learning difficulties, while yet others have average or excellent language skills and average or even high IQ.

What all individuals on the autism spectrum share in common are social communication difficulties (both are disabilities), difficulties adjusting to unexpected change (another disability), a love of repetition or "need for sameness," unusually narrow interests, and sensory hyper- and hypo-sensitivities (all examples of difference). Autism can also be associated with cognitive strengths and even talents, notably in attention to and memory for detail, and a strong drive to detect patterns (all of these are differences). How these are manifested is likely to be strongly influenced by language and IQ.

The other source of the huge heterogeneity is that autism is frequently accompanied by co-occurring conditions. I mentioned gastrointestinal pain or epilepsy (both examples of disorders and sometimes diseases), dyspraxia, ADHD and dyslexia (all examples of disabilities), and anxiety and depression (both examples of mental health conditions). This is just a partial list. A recent study shows that 50 percent of autistic people have at least four such co-occurring conditions (including language disorder or learning difficulties), and more than 95 percent of autistic children have at least one condition in addition to autism.

The relevance of this for the neurodiversity debate is that if we dip into the wide range of features that are seen in autism, we will find differences and disabilities (both compatible with the neurodiversity framework), and we will find examples of disorders and even diseases, which are more compatible with a medical than a neurodiversity model.

Regarding scientific evidence, there is evidence for both neurodiversity and disorder. For example, at the genetic level, about 5 to15 percent of the variance in autism can be attributed to rare genetic variants/mutations, many of which cause not just autism but also severe developmental delays (disorder), while about 10 to 50 percent of the variance in autism can be attributed to common genetic variants such as single nucleotide polymorphisms (SNPs), which simply reflect individual differences or natural variation.

At the neural level, some regions of the autistic brain (such as the amygdala, in childhood) are larger, and others (such as the posterior section of the corpus callosum) are smaller. These are evidence of difference but not necessarily disorder. Early brain overgrowth is another sign of difference but not necessarily disorder.

Post-mortem studies of the autistic brain reveal a greater number of neurons in the frontal lobe, suggesting that there may be reduced apoptosis (or pruning of of neural connections) in autism, but again this may just be evidence for difference rather than disorder. Against this, structural differences in the language areas of the brain in autistic individuals who are minimally verbal are likely to be a sign of disorder.

Functional MRI (fMRI) studies at times show less or more brain activity during different tasks, and again this can be interpreted in terms of difference and disability, but not clearly evidence of disorder. On the other hand, where autistic individuals have demonstrable epilepsy with a clear electrophysiological signature, this is a sign of disorder or even disease.

At the behavioral and cognitive levels autistic people show both differences, signs of disability and disorder. For example, young autistic toddlers may look for longer at nonsocial stimuli than at social stimuli, and autistic people may show their best performance on IQ tests on the Block Design subtest, perhaps reflecting their strong aptitude for attention to detail and disassembling complex information into its component parts.

Both of these are simply differences, compatible with the neurodiversity model. Aspects of social cognition reflect areas of disability in autism, and are often the reason for why they seek and receive a diagnosis. But if an autistic person has severe learning difficulties or is minimally verbal (defined as having fewer than 30 words), this is arguably beyond neurodiversity and more compatible with the medical model.

In sum, there is a case for all of the terms "disorder," "disability," "difference" and "disease" being applicable to different forms of autism or to the co-occurring conditions. Neurodiversity is a fact of nature; our brains are all different. So there is no point in being a neurodiversity denier, any more than being a biodiversity denier. But by taking a fine-grained look at the heterogeneity within autism we can see how sometimes the neurodiversity model fits autism very well, and that sometimes the disorder/medical model is a better explanation.

What is attractive about the neurodiversity model is that it doesn't pathologize and focus disproportionately on what the person struggles with, and instead takes a more balanced view, to give equal attention to what the person can do. In addition it recognizes that genetic or other kinds of biological variation are intrinsic to people's identity, their sense of self and personhood, which should be given equal respect alongside any other form of diversity, such as gender. But to encompass the breadth of the autism spectrum, we need to make space for the medical model too.

The views expressed are those of the author(s) and are not necessarily those of Scientific American.

About the Author

Simon Baron-Cohen is director of the Autism Research Center at the University of Cambridge, UK, and president of the International Society for Autism Research.

Clearing Up Some Misconceptions about Neurodiversity

By Aiyana Bailin

To my dismay, Simon Baron-Cohen's recent article "The Concept of Neurodiversity is Dividing the Autism Community" perpetuates a common misunderstanding of the neurodiversity movement: that it views autism as a difference but not a disability. Baron-Cohen presents the issue as one of opposing sides: the medical model, which sees autism as a set of symptoms and deficits to be cured or treated, and the neurodiversity model, which he believes ignores any disabling aspects of autism. Unfortunately, this confuses the neurodiversity movement with the social model of disability, and it is an incomplete understanding of the social model at that.

Before I go into details, let me summarize what the neurodiversity movement *does* believe:

- Autism and other neurological variations (learning disabilities, ADHD, etc.) may be disabilities, but they are not flaws. People with neurological differences are not broken or incomplete versions of normal people.
- Disability, no matter how profound, does not diminish personhood. People with atypical brains are fully human, with inalienable human rights, just like everyone else.
- People with disabilities can live rich, meaningful lives.
- Neurological variations are a vital part of humanity, as much as variations in size, shape, skin color and personality. None of us has the right (or the wisdom) to try and improve upon our species by deciding which characteristics to keep and which to discard. Every person is valuable.
- Disability is a complicated thing. Often, it's defined more by society's expectations than by individual conditions. Not always, but often.

The social model of disability comes from the field of disability studies. It says that a person is "disabled" when the (societal) environment doesn't accommodate their needs. An example: in a world where ramps and elevators are everywhere, a wheelchair user isn't "disabled," because he/she/they can access all the same things as a person who walks: schools, jobs, restaurants, etc. However, providing equal opportunity doesn't mean ignoring the differences and difficulties a wheelchair user may experience.

In the 2004 article "The Right Not to Work: Power and Disability," Sunny Taylor explains: "The state of being mentally or physically challenged is what [disability theorists] term being impaired; with impairment comes personal challenges and drawbacks in terms of mental processes and physical mobility.... Disability, in contrast, is the political and social repression of impaired people. This is accomplished by making them economically and socially isolated. Disabled people have limited housing options, are socially and culturally ostracized, and have very few career opportunities."

Few (if any) neurodiversity advocates deny that impairments exist in autism. Or that some impairments are more challenging than others, with or without accommodations. We, like Baron-Cohen, hope to solve the health struggles that often come with autism, such as epilepsy and digestive issues. But while these are more common among autistic people than nonautistic (or "neurotypical") people, they aren't actually symptoms of autism.

And culture affects these things, too. Depending on time and place in history, epilepsy could make a person a respected shaman or suspected of demonic possession. Gluten allergies are much easier to accommodate now than they were 20 years ago before food companies started offering gluten-free options. If wheat and rye went extinct, gluten allergy would never be a disability again!

When we talk about "not pathologizing autism," we don't mean "pretending autistic people don't have impairments." But we also don't assume that neurological and behavioral differences are always problems. For example, there's nothing inherently wrong with disliking social activities. Not wanting to socialize is different from wanting to participate and being unable to. Both are possibilities for autistic people. One requires acceptance, the other requires assistance. Sadly, I have yet to meet a therapist who doesn't treat the two as equivalent and in equal need of correction.

While there is a lot of overlap with the social model, the neurodiversity approach is primarily a call to include and respect people whose brains work in atypical ways, regardless of their level of disability (I will focus here on autism, but neurodiversity is about "all kinds of minds"). This requires challenging our assumptions about what's normal, what's necessary and what's desirable for a person to live well. Of course, better accommodations and reduced stigma would improve our lives immensely. But so would a broader definition of a meaningful life. As Taylor puts it: "Western culture has a very limited idea of what being useful to society is. People can be useful in ways other than monetarily."

The neurodiversity movement believes in giving autistic people the tools to succeed in the workplace, but not shaming or pitying those who will never be financially (or physically) independent. We believe that a person who needs lifelong care can also be happy and reach personal goals. Taylor adds, "Independence is perhaps prized beyond all else in this country, and for disabled people this means that our lives are automatically seen as tragically dependent."

But is independence really about being able to brush your own teeth, or is it more about being able to choose your own friends? Disability theorists and neurodiversity advocates think the second is far more important. Most therapies, however, teach only concrete practical skills, not personal empowerment.

When we say "Autism is just another way of being human," we mean that profound impairments don't change a person's right to dignity, to privacy and to as much self-determination as possible, whether that means choosing their career or choosing their clothes. I cringe to see how often autistic people get videoed at their worst, without their consent, and broadcast on the internet for the world to see. You would probably be furious if someone did that with your moments of deepest personal struggle! The fact that these kids (and adults) can't speak up doesn't mean they're okay with it. Inability to answer is not consent. Additionally, autistic children are regularly subjected to therapies that teach them to hide their discomforts, stifle their personalities and be more obedient (or "compliant") than their neurotypical peers, putting them at increased risk of bullying and sexual abuse.

Respecting neurodiversity means respecting nonverbal choices, even when those choices are "weird" or "not age-appropriate." It means respecting the word "no," whether it's spoken, signed, or shown by behavior. It's giving the same attention to a person using an AAC (augmentative and alternative communication) device that we give when a person speaks verbally. It's understanding that muting an AAC device is the moral equivalent of taping over the mouth of a child who communicates by speaking. It means not using high-pitched baby talk with a 10-year-old, even if that 10-year-old still wears diapers and puts sand in his mouth. It's never letting a child overhear herself described as "such hard work" or "a pity" or "a puzzle" or "so far behind," no matter how little she appears to understand. Inability to respond doesn't mean inability to comprehend, as we've heard many times from self-advocates like Carly Fleischmann and Ido Kedar.

Baron-Cohen mentions "social difficulties" as a disability in autism, and for many autistic people, their social struggles are indeed disabling. But that's an incomplete picture. Some autistic people genuinely prefer their own company. Many autistic people socialize better with other autistic people than with typical peers, so perhaps we shouldn't judge their social skills solely on their interactions with neurotypicals. And, perhaps most importantly, one of the biggest social difficulties faced by autistic people is neurotypical people's reluctance to interact with those they perceive as "different."

That's a social problem caused *for* autistic people *by* nonautistic people, not a social disability in autism. Asking only autistic people to change how they socialize is like asking minorities to speak and dress more like white people in order to be accepted. That's a really bad way to combat prejudice, racial or neurological.

More people now use the language of neurodiversity, talking about accepting and supporting autistic differences. Unfortunately, however they phrase it, most autism therapies still uphold "more typical behavior" as the gold standard of success. Even though numerous autistic adults warn that the strain of faking normality often leads to depression, burnout and even regression later, years after the therapy was declared a success. Respecting neurodiversity means not insisting on eye contact, when autistic people have stated (over and over and over) that eye contact is so hard, so overwhelming and so stressful that it destroys their ability to pay attention.

The same goes for "quiet hands" or any time an autistic child is forced to act more typical at the expense of energy they need for intellectual development or personal growth. Studies are finally confirming what autistic people have said for decades: we get better outcomes when it's the caregivers rather than the children who are taught to behave differently. It's tragic how often the autistic viewpoint is ignored by researchers and therapy companies.

Thinking in terms of neurodiversity means challenging the assumption that pretend play is necessary just because it's what neurotypical children do. While typical children learn with a hands-on, stepwise approach, many autistic children learn best by observing for a long time before trying a new skill. Just as visual learners or auditory learners should be allowed to use the learning method that works best for them, so too should autistic children. We should respect that they usually learn things in a different order than typical kids do, and stop tracking their progress on neurotypical developmental timelines.

I'm a respite carer. I've had clients on the spectrum (and with other developmental disabilities) from ages four to the early 20s. Many are nonverbal or minimally verbal. I believe all are intelligent in their own ways, even if they have intellectual disabilities. I have clients who melt down or blow up. I sympathize with their frustrations. I have clients who bite themselves or me. I'm certain that they never do so without reason. I have clients who communicate with single words, apps, drawings or simply pulling me to what they want. I don't want to change their communication style; I want to learn it like a second language. I have clients who will "pass" as nonautistic, and clients who will probably never live on their own. I make no assumptions about who will have a more fulfilling or enjoyable life.

There are struggles that come with being far from "normal" and struggles that come with being almost "normal"—not to mention, typical lives are hardly free of challenges! Struggle is part of everyone's life, not just disabled people's. Many of us assume we know what a good life looks like, but we're very limited by our own experiences. A good life means different things to different people. Just ask a Syrian refugee and a New York socialite what they need to be happy.

My clients are complicated, just like all human beings. I have clients who do gross and socially inappropriate things in public. If I am embarrassed by their actions, that's my problem, not theirs. I have clients who gently stroke my hair with shaky hands, who silently share their favorite foods with me, who flap and jump and screech with excitement when I arrive at their door. I wouldn't trade their flapping hands and shining eyes for anything in the world. Their very existence is beautiful.

My clients usually have impairments. My clients are often disabled. My clients are all cool and interesting people. Some of my clients notice things others miss. Some communicate eloquently without language. Some make jokes using only one or two words. Some have skills in memory, engineering and music that make me envious. You might be very surprised by which descriptions belong to which clients.

Respecting neurodiversity means challenging assumptions about what intelligence is and how to measure it. It means reminding ourselves that just because a person can't speak doesn't mean they aren't listening. It means not asking someone to prove their intelligence before talking to them in an age-appropriate way or offering them intellectually stimulating opportunities. It means remembering that there can be a huge disconnect between mind and body, and that a person's actions may not reflect their intentions, especially when they are overwhelmed or upset.

Respecting neurodiversity means the professional community needs to apologize for decades of mistakenly insisting that autistic people lack emotions or empathy, and for all the harm, both physical and psychological, that has been done to autistic people (and is still being done) because of those errors made by neurotypical observers. It means asking whether some "weaknesses" are really strengths in disguise. It means always asking "Is this activity/skill/behavioral goal actually necessary, or just normal?" and "What can we adults do differently so our kids don't have to?"

I suspect parents are thinking, "But I have to teach my child how to get along in this world! I might be willing to change for them, but other people won't." Yes, you can work to teach your child the rules of your society, without letting those lessons take over their life. Children at school have to raise their hands and wait to speak, but we don't require this at home. Practicing an instrument is exhausting, so we don't ask young children to do it for hours at a time. Treat "acting normal" the same way.

It's work, and hard work at that. Don't ask for it all the time. Acknowledge that it's usually difficult and sometimes downright painful. Ask yourself what you'd allow done to a nondisabled child. Would you let a therapist physically restrain her for biting her nails? Hide his favorite food until he cooperates? If it's not okay for a neurotypical child, it's not okay for an autistic one.

Respecting neurodiversity means listening to autistic adults and taking them seriously when they tell us that the psychological cost of fitting in usually outweighs the benefits. It means accepting that some kids will learn to write but never talk, or will always understand music better than manners, or will never have an interest in sports, or don't identify with a binary gender; and that there is room in this world to appreciate and celebrate all these individuals for who they are, regardless of how much help they need. Doing so makes their world, and ours, a better place.

The views expressed are those of the author(s) and are not necessarily those of Scientific American.

About the Author

Aiyana Bailin is an autism care professional and disability rights advocate. She blogs at https://restlesshands42.wordpress.com.

The Neurodiversity Movement Should Acknowledge Autism as a Medical Disability

By Yuval Levental

Aiyana Bailin, a disability rights advocate, wrote a response titled "Clearing Up Some Misconceptions about Neurodiversity," where she claims that while she supports neurodiversity, she believes that autism is best understood through the social model of disability. This means that the negative aspects of autism are caused by a lack of external accommodations, such as in improper work environments.

Advocating for medical research, former president of Autism Speaks Liz Feld has stated that one third of people with autism also have a seizure disorder, half suffer serious digestive complications, 49 percent wander, and more than 30 percent are nonverbal. Feld claims that no accommodation could solve those specific difficulties, and that they interfere with their quality of life. In 2018, the National Council on Severe Autism was founded to take action regarding those concerns, with its founder, Jill Escher, stating that "For countless families devoted to the well-being of their disabled loved ones, the daily challenges can be overwhelming, and the prospects for the future extremely bleak."

Many who view autism as a difference or through the social model of disability claim that those issues are co-occurring conditions and not part of autism. However, as of now, there is no evidence that those conditions can be separated from a person's autism. Furthermore, those perspectives don't give a clear portrayal of how autism should be defined. As Jill Escher said in a blog post on this issue, "If my kids don't have autism, what do they have?"

Furthermore, a study in 2015 concluded that compared to individuals with other disabilities, young people with autism have significantly higher rates of unemployment and social isolation. This study also included many people with milder variants of autism.

There are some success stories of high-functioning individuals being able to find jobs through autism hiring programs; however, this success is quite rare. For instance, Microsoft only hired five candidates in one session of its autism hiring program. This is because accommodations are simply to aid a person in working, but the essential job requirements should be the same.

One way to solve this dilemma is to push for more medical research to find the causes of autism, while acknowledging that autism shouldn't have to define a person's identity. Given the aforementioned difficulties, there is no reason why a person has to be completely dependent on having autism to have a sense of self-worth. As Thomas Clements, who is an autism advocate, wrote: "My Asperger's is a part of me, even if the social difficulties it entails limit me in my interactions a lot of the time. But I am worried that the fringe elements of the social justice and neurodiversity movements are prone to fanaticism and will insist that any hint of treatment or alteration of the sacred autistic 'identity' is somehow '*fascist*' or '*eugenicist*'."

The views expressed are those of the author(s) and are not necessarily those of Scientific American.

About the Author

Yuval Levental is an autistic individual who critically analyzes autism advocacy.

Are Geeky Couples More Likely to Have Kids with Autism?

By Simon Baron-Cohen

In 1997 my colleague Sally Wheelwright and I conducted a study involving nearly 2,000 families in the U.K. We included about half these families because they had at least one child with autism, a developmental condition in which individuals have difficulty communicating and interacting with others and display obsessive behaviors. The other families had children with a diagnosis of Tourette's syndrome, Down syndrome or language delays but not autism. We asked parents in each family a simple question: What was their job? Many mothers had not worked outside the home, so we could not use their data, but the results from fathers were intriguing: 12.5 percent of fathers of children with autism were engineers, compared with only 5 percent of fathers of children without autism.

Likewise, 21.2 percent of grandfathers of children with autism had been engineers, compared with only 2.5 percent of grandfathers of children without autism. The pattern appeared on both sides of the family. Women who had a child with autism were more likely to have a father who had been an engineer–and they were more likely to have married someone whose father had been an engineer.

Coincidence? I think not.

A possible explanation involves a phenomenon known as assortative mating, which usually means "like pairs with like." I first encountered the concept in an undergraduate statistics tutorial at the University of Oxford in 1978, when my tutor told me (perhaps to make statistics a little more lively) that whom you have sex with is not random. When I asked her to elaborate, she gave me the example of height: tall people tend to mate with tall people, and short people tend to mate with short people. Height is not the only characteristic that consciously and subconsciously influences partner selection–

age is another example, as are personality types. Now, more than 30 years later, my colleagues and I are testing whether assortative mating explains why autism persists in the general population. When people with technical minds—such as engineers, scientists, computer programmers and mathematicians—marry other technical-minded individuals, or their sons and daughters do, do they pass down linked groups of genes that not only endow their progeny with useful cognitive talents but also increase their children's chances of developing autism?

System Check

I began studying autism in the 1980s. By then, the psychogenic theory of autism—which argued that emotionally disinterested mothers caused their children's autism—had been soundly refuted. Michael Rutter, now at King's College London, and others had begun to study autism in twins and had shown that autism was highly heritable. Genetics, not parenting, was at work.

Today researchers know that an identical twin of someone with autism is around 70 times more likely to develop autism, too, compared with an unrelated individual. Although researchers have uncovered associations between specific genes and autism, no one has identified a group of genes that reliably predicts who will develop the condition. The genetics of autism are far more complex than that. What I have been interested in understanding, however, is how genes for autism survive in the first place. After all, autism limits one's abilities to read others' emotions and to form relationships, which in turn may reduce one's chances of having children and passing on one's genes.

One possibility is that the genes responsible for autism persist, generation after generation, because they are co-inherited with genes underlying certain cognitive talents common to both people with autism and technical-minded people whom some might call geeks. In essence, some geeks may be carriers of genes for autism: in their own life, they do not demonstrate any signs of severe autism, but when they pair up and have kids, their children may get a double dose of autism genes and traits. In this way, assortative mating between technical-minded people might spread autism genes.

Because "geek" is not the most scientific term, and for some may be pejorative, I needed to formulate a more precise definition of the cognitive talents shared by technical-minded people and people with autism. In the early 2000s Wheelwright and I surveyed nearly 100 families with at least one child with autism and asked another basic question: What was their child's obsession? We received a diverse array of answers that included memorizing train timetables, learning the names of every member of a category (for instance, dinosaurs, cars, mushrooms), putting electrical switches around the house into particular positions, and running the water in the sink and rushing outside to see it flowing out of the drainpipe.

On the surface, these very different behaviors seem to share little, but they are all examples of systemizing. I define systemizing as the drive to analyze or construct a system—a mechanical system (such as a car or computer), a natural system (nutrition) or an abstract system (mathematics). Systemizing is not restricted to technology, engineering and math. Some systems are even social, such as a business, and some involve artistic pursuits, such as classical dance or piano. All systems follow rules. When you systemize, you identify the rules that govern the system so you can predict how that system works. This fundamental drive to systemize might explain why people with autism love repetition and resist unexpected changes.

Collaborating once again with Wheelwright, who is now at the University of Southampton in England, I put the link between systemizing and autism to the test. We found that children with Asperger's syndrome—a form of autism with no language or intelligence impairments—outperformed older, typically developing children on a test of understanding mechanics. We also found that on average, adults and children with Asperger's scored higher on self-report and parent-report measures of systemizing. Finally, we found that people with Asperger's scored higher on a test of attention to detail. Attention to detail is a prerequisite for good systemizing.

It makes a world of difference when trying to understand a system if you spot the small details or if you mistake one tiny variable in the system. (Imagine getting one digit wrong in a math calculation.) When we gave the test of attention to detail to parents, both the mothers and fathers of children with autism were also faster and more accurate than those of typically developing children.

Engineers aren't the only technical-minded people who might harbor autism genes. In 1998 Wheelwright and I found that math students at the University of Cambridge were nine times more likely than humanities students to report having a formal diagnosis of autism, including Asperger's, which will be folded into the broader "autism spectrum disorder" in the newest edition of psychiatry's guidebook, the DSM-5. Whereas only 0.2 percent of students in the humanities had autism, a figure not so different from the rate of autism reported in the wider population at the time, 1.8 percent of the math students had it. We also found that the siblings of mathematicians were five times more likely to have autism, compared with the siblings of those in the humanities.

In another test of the link between autism and math, Wheelwright and I developed a metric for measuring traits associated with autism in the general population, called the Autism Spectrum Quotient (AQ). It has 50 items, each representing one such trait. No one scores zero on the test. On average, typically developing men score 17 out of 50, and typically developing women score 15 out of 50. People with autism usually score above 32. We gave the AQ to winners of the British Mathematical Olympiad. They averaged 21 out of 50. This pattern suggested that–regardless of official diagnoses–mathematical talent was also linked to a higher number of traits associated with autism.

The Silicon Valley Phenomenon

One way to test the assortative mating theory is to compare couples in which both individuals are strong systemizers with couples who include only one strong systemizer–or none. Two-systemizer couples may be more likely to have a child with autism. My colleagues and

I created a Web site where parents can report what they studied in college, their occupations, and whether or not their children have autism (www.cambridgepsychology.com/graduateparents).

Meanwhile we are exploring the theory from other angles. If genes for technical aptitude are linked to genes for autism, then autism should be more common in places around the world where many systemizers live, work and marry–places such as Silicon Valley in California, which some people claim has autism rates 10 times higher than the average for the general population.

In Bangalore, the Silicon Valley of India, local clinicians have made similar observations. Alumni of the Massachusetts Institute of Technology have also reported rates of autism 10 times higher than average among their children. Unfortunately, no one has yet conducted detailed and systematic studies in Silicon Valley, Bangalore or M.I.T., so these accounts remain anecdotal.

My colleagues and I, however, have investigated the rates of autism in Eindhoven, the Silicon Valley of the Netherlands. Royal Philips Electronics has been a major employer in Eindhoven since 1891, and IBM has a branch in the city. Indeed, some 30 percent of jobs in Eindhoven are in the IT sector. Eindhoven is also home to Eindhoven University of Technology and High Tech Campus Eindhoven, the Dutch equivalent of M.I.T. We compared rates of autism in Eindhoven with rates of autism in two similarly sized cities in the Netherlands: Utrecht and Haarlem.

In 2010 we asked every school in all three cities to count how many children among their pupils had a formal diagnosis of autism. A total of 369 schools took part, providing information on about 62,505 children. We found that the rate of autism in Eindhoven was almost three times higher (229 per 10,000) than in Haarlem (84 per 10,000) or Utrecht (57 per 10,000).

Male Minds

In parallel with testing the link between autism and systemizing, we have been examining why autism appears to be so much more common among boys than among girls. In classic autism, the sex ratio is about four boys to every girl. In Asperger's, the sex ratio may be as high as nine boys for every girl.

Likewise, strong systemizing is much more common in men than in women. In childhood, boys on average show a stronger interest in mechanical systems (such as toy vehicles) and constructional systems (such as Lego). In adulthood, men are overrepresented in STEM subjects (*s*cience, *t*echnology, *e*ngineering and *m*ath) but not in people-centered sciences such as clinical psychology or medicine. We have been investigating whether high levels of the hormone testosterone in the fetus, long known to play a role in "masculinizing" the developing brain in animals, correlate with strong systemizing and more traits associated with autism. A human male fetus produces at least twice as much testosterone as a female fetus does.

To test these ideas, my colleague Bonnie Auyeung of the Cambridge Autism Research Center and I studied 235 pregnant women undergoing amniocentesis–a procedure in which a long needle samples the amniotic fluid surrounding a fetus. We found that the more testosterone surrounding a fetus in the womb, the stronger the children's later interest in systems, the better their attention to detail and the higher their number of traits associated with autism. Researchers in Cambridge, England, and Denmark are now collaborating to test whether children who eventually develop autism were exposed to elevated levels of testosterone in the womb.

If fetal testosterone plays an important role in autism, women with autism should be especially masculinized in certain ways. Some evidence suggests that this is true. Girls with autism show "tomboyism" in their toy-choice preferences. On average, women with autism and their mothers also have an elevated rate of polycystic ovary syndrome, which is caused by excess testosterone and involves irregular menstrual cycles, delayed onset of puberty and hirsutism (excessive body hair).

Prenatal testosterone, if it is involved in autism, is not acting alone. It behaves epigenetically, changing gene expression, and interacts with other important molecules. Similarly, the link between autism and systemizing, if confirmed through further studies, is unlikely to account for the full complexity of autism genetics. And we should not draw the simplistic conclusion that all technical-minded people carry genes for autism.

Investigating why certain communities have higher rates of autism, and whether genes that contribute to the condition are linked to genes for technical aptitude, may help us understand why the human brain sometimes develops differently than usual. People with autism, whose minds differ from what we consider typical, frequently display both disability and exceptional aptitude. Genes that contribute to autism may overlap with genes for the uniquely human ability to understand how the world works in extraordinary detail—to see beauty in patterns inherent in nature, technology, music and math.

Referenced

The Essential Difference: The Truth about the Male and Female Brain. Simon Baron-Cohen. Basic Books, 2004.

Sex Differences in the Brain: Implications for Explaining Autism. Simon Baron-Cohen et al. in Science, Vol. 310, pages 819–823; November 4, 2005.

Autism and Asperger Syndrome: The Facts. Simon Baron-Cohen. Oxford University Press, 2008.

Why Are Autism Spectrum Conditions More Prevalent in Males? Simon Baron-Cohen et al. in PloS Biology, Vol. 9, No. 6, Article No. e1001081; June 14, 2011.

About the Author

Simon Baron-Cohen is professor of developmental psychopathology at the University of Cambridge and director of the Autism Research Center. He is author of The Essential Difference *(Basic Books, 2004), among other books.*

How Big Data Are Unlocking the Mysteries of Autism

By Wendy Chung

When I started my pediatric genetic practice over 20 years ago, I was frustrated by constantly having to tell families and patients that I couldn't answer many of their questions about autism and what the future held for them. What were the causes of their child's particular behavioral and medical challenges? Would their child talk? Have seizures? What I did know was that research was the key to unlocking the mysteries of a remarkably heterogeneous disorder that affects more than five million Americans and has no FDA-approved treatments. Now, thanks in large part to the impact of genetic research, those answers are starting to come into focus.

Five years ago we launched SPARK (Simons Foundation Powering Autism Research for Knowledge) to harness the power of big data by engaging hundreds of thousands of individuals with autism and their family members to participate in research. The more people who participate, the deeper and richer these data sets become, catalyzing research that is expanding our knowledge of both biology and behavior to develop more precise approaches to medical and behavioral issues.

SPARK is the world's largest autism research study to date with over 250,000 participants, more than 100,000 of whom have provided DNA samples through the simple act of spitting in a tube. We have generated genomic data that have been de-identified and made available to qualified researchers. SPARK has itself been able to analyze 19,000 genes to find possible connections to autism; worked with 31 of the nation's leading medical schools and autism research centers; and helped thousands of participating families enroll in nearly 100 additional autism research studies.

Genetic research has taught us that what we commonly call autism is actually a spectrum of hundreds of conditions that vary widely among adults and children. Across this spectrum, individuals share core symptoms and challenges with social interaction, restricted interests and/or repetitive behaviors.

We now know that genes play a central role in the causes of these "autisms," which are the result of genetic changes in combination with other causes including prenatal factors. To date, research employing data science and machine learning has identified approximately 150 genes related to autism, but suggests there may be as many as 500 or more. Finding additional genes and commonalities among individuals who share similar genetic differences is crucial to advancing autism research and developing improved supports and treatments. Essentially, we will take a page from the playbook that oncologists use to treat certain types of cancer based upon their genetic signatures and apply targeted therapeutic strategies to help people with autism.

But in order to get answers faster and be certain of these results, SPARK and our research partners need a huge sample size: "bigger data." To ensure an accurate inventory of all the major genetic contributors, and learn if and how different genetic variants contribute to autistic behaviors, we need not only the largest but also the most diverse group of participants.

The genetic, medical and behavioral data SPARK collects from people with autism and their families is rich in detail and can be leveraged by many different investigators. Access to rich data sets draws talented scientists to the field of autism science to develop new methods of finding patterns in the data, better predicting associated behavioral and medical issues, and, perhaps, identifying more effective supports and treatments.

Genetic research is already providing answers and insights about prognosis. For example, one SPARK family's genetic result is strongly associated with a lack of spoken language but an ability to understand language. Armed with this information, the medical team provided the child with an assistive communication device that decreased tantrums that arose from the child's frustration at being unable to express himself. An adult who was diagnosed at age 11 with a form of autism that used to be known as Asperger's syndrome recently learned that the cause of her autism is *KMT2C*-related syndrome, a rare genetic disorder caused by changes in the gene *KMT2C*.

Some genetic syndromes associated with autism also confer cancer risks, so receiving these results is particularly important. We have returned genetic results to families with mutations in PTEN, which is associated with a higher risk of breast, thyroid, kidney and uterine cancer. A genetic diagnosis means that they can now be screened earlier and more frequently for specific cancers.

In other cases, SPARK has identified genetic causes of autism that can be treated. Through whole exome sequencing, SPARK identified a case of phenylketonuria (PKU) that was missed during newborn screening. This inherited disorder causes a buildup of amino acid in the blood, which can cause behavior and movement problems, seizures and developmental disabilities. With this knowledge, the family started their child on treatment with a specialized diet including low levels of phenylalanine.

Today, thanks to a growing community of families affected by autism who, literally, give a part of themselves to help understand the vast complexities of autism, I can tell about 10 percent of parents what genetic change caused their child's autism.

We know that big data, with each person representing their unique profile of someone impacted by autism, will lead to many of the answers we seek. Better genetic insights, gleaned through complex analysis of rich data, will help provide the means to support individuals–children and adults across the spectrum–through early intervention, assistive communication, tailored education and, someday, genetically-based treatments. We strive to enable every person with autism to be the best possible version of themselves.

This is an opinion and analysis article.

About the Author

Wendy Chung, M.D., Ph.D., is principal investigator for SPARK (Simons Foundation Powering Autism Research for Knowledge); the Kennedy Family

Professor of Pediatrics and Medicine at Columbia University Vagelos College of Physicians and Surgeons; and a clinical and molecular geneticist and physician at New York-Presbyterian/Columbia University Irving Medical Center. In 2020, she was elected to membership in the National Academy of Medicine.

Section 4: Life on the Spectrum

Autistic People Make Great Social Partners if You Actually Give Them a Chance

By Scott Barry Kaufman

For many years, researchers have treated the individual traits and characteristics of autistic people as an enduring essence of their autism—in isolation of the social context and without even asking autistic people what their social life is actually like. However, perspective matters. Who is to say it's autistic people who are the "awkward" ones?

A number of myths about autistic people abound. For one, it's a great myth that autistic people lack empathy. This is how they were depicted for so many years in the clinical literature and in the media—as emotionless, socially clueless robots. However, the more you get to know an autistic person, the more you realize just how caring they can be, even though they may have some difficulties reading social cues. As Steve Silberman points out, empathy is a two-way street.

Another common misconception is that autistic people aren't social. I really like some recent approaches that add greater complexity to this issue, showing that when you take a contextual strengths-based approach you can see that people on the autism spectrum are much more social than researchers ever realized. The lens upon which we look at a person matters. As Megan Clark and Dawn Adams put it, "When autism is viewed through a deficit lens the strengths, positive attributes and interests of individuals on the spectrum can be overshadowed."

In one recent study, Clark and Adams asked 83 children on the autism spectrum (aged 8 to 15 years) various questions about themselves. When asked, "What do you like most about yourself?" the most common themes were, "I am a good friend or person to be around" and "I am good at particular things." When asked,

"What do you enjoy the most?" one of the most endorsed themes was social interaction.

In other words, when asked to talk about their own lives, social interactions organically emerged as a prominent positive theme among autistic adults. Clark and Adams concluded that "self-report studies provide individuals on the autism spectrum with a much-needed opportunity to express and share their attributes, strengths and interests with others, adding their voice to the literature." I consider this a step forward–actually asking them about their lives, not just scientists telling autistic people what they are like.

This research is consistent with research showing that at least 80% of children on the autism spectrum have at least one friend and the majority are satisfied with their friendships. While it is true that children on the autism spectrum in general education classrooms are often on the periphery of their classroom social engagement, researchers suggest it's due in large part to the lack of supports that would allow autistic people to engage with their peers on the school playground.

Bias may be a significant factor in allowing us to see the real social potential of autistic people. In one study, Noah Sasson and colleagues found that even within a couple seconds typically developing people make quick judgments about people on the autism spectrum. These patterns are robust, happen quickly, and persist across child and adult age groups. Unfortunately, these judgments are not favorable or kind.

But here's the kicker: the researchers found that the biases against autistic people *disappeared* when the impressions were based on conversational content lacking audio-visual cues. As the researchers note, "style, not substance drives negative impressions of people on the ASD." They advocate for a broader perspective that considers both the impairments and biases of potential social partners.

Enter a more recent study. Kerianne Morrison and colleagues looked at the real time social interactions of 67 autistic adults and 56 typically developing adults. The participants engaged in one of three conversational groups: autism-autism, typically developing-typically developing, and autism-typically developing. After the conversation was over, the participants recorded their impressions of their partner and the quality of the interaction. This allowed the researchers to separate impression information from ratings of the actual quality of the conversation.

Autistic adults were perceived to be more awkward, less attractive, and less warm compared to typically developing social partners. However, autistic adults were *not* rated as less intelligent, trustworthy, or likeable. Also, despite the autistic adults being rated as more awkward and less attractive, perception of the *quality* of the conversation did not differ between the autistic adults and the typically developing social partners. This finding replicates the 2017 study that negative impressions of autistic people in social situation is driven more by their presentation differences rather than the actual content of their conversation.

Also, compared to typically developing participants, the researchers found that autistic participants reported feeling closer to their social partners. There are multiple possible explanations but one may be that autistic people value social interactions more, especially when given the chance to socialize. Perhaps people on the autism spectrum are more inclined to shun small talk and superficial banter and appreciate more close relationships than typically developing people. At least in the mating domain, there is evidence that people with autistic-like traits tend to be less interested in short-term mating, and report a stronger commitment to long-term romantic relationships. Not only can autistic people make great social partners, but they can also make great romantic partners!

Finally, Kerianne Morrison and colleagues found a trend for autistic adults to prefer interacting with other autistic adults, and autistic people reported disclosing more about themselves when interacting with another autistic person compared to when interacting with a typically developing social partner. Zooming in on the content of the conversations, autistic individuals were more likely to geek out over their special interest areas when chatting with others on the autism spectrum. The researchers conclude: "these results suggest that social affiliation may increase for autistic adults when partnered with other autistic people, and support reframing social interaction difficulties in autism as a relational rather than individual impairment."

I really like the idea of reframing social awkwardness in autism. As I suggested elsewhere, perhaps we should think about the social style of autistic people as a form of *social creativity*. An emerging class of "drama-based group interventions" are applying drama-based techniques in a group setting to increase joint engagement and play among autistic children.

For instance, Matthew Lerner and his colleagues have used improvisation techniques to teach autistic children how to respond to unexpected social scenarios. The activities are designed to be fun and to provide shared joy and connection among the participants. Many of the autistic children who participate are treated as "awkward" and "weird" by others at schools. However, when they engage in improv with each other they are viewed as the funny, quirky, awesome human beings that they really truly are.

All of these findings suggest that the social interaction difficulties seen among autistic people may be highly contextual and dependent on the right fit between the person and the environment. But even more broadly, these new methods and approaches within psychology are transforming how autistic people think of themselves in the world and what they are ultimately able to become. It highlights the way their unique brain wiring can be a strength, instead of immediately trying to "fix" them. By meeting autistic people where they are, we see that they are capable of far more than researchers and the general public had long believed to be the case.

The views expressed are those of the author(s) and are not necessarily those of Scientific American.

About the Author

Scott Barry Kaufman, Ph.D., is a humanistic psychologist exploring the depths of human potential. He has taught courses on intelligence, creativity, and well-being at Columbia University, NYU, the University of Pennsylvania, and elsewhere. He hosts The Psychology Podcast, and is author and/or editor of 9 books, including Transcend: The New Science of Self-Actualization, Wired to Create: Unravelling the Mysteries of the Creative Mind *(with Carolyn Gregoire), and* Ungifted: Intelligence Redefined. *In 2015, he was named one of "50 Groundbreaking Scientists who are changing the way we see the world" by* Business Insider. *Find out more at http://ScottBarryKaufman.com. He wrote the extremely popular* Beautiful Minds *blog for* Scientific American *for close to a decade.*

Autism—It's Different in Girls

By Maia Szalavitz

When Frances was an infant, she was late to babble, walk and talk. She was three before she would respond to her own name. Although there were hints that something was unusual about her development, the last thing her parents suspected was autism. "She was very social and a very happy, easy baby," says Kevin Pelphrey, Frances's father.

Pelphrey is a leading autism researcher at Yale University's world-renowned Child Study Center. But even he did not recognize the condition in his daughter, who was finally diagnosed at about five years of age. Today Frances is a slender, lightly freckled 12-year-old with her dad's warm brown eyes. Like many girls her age, she is shy but also has strong opinions about what she does and does not want. At lunchtime, she and her little brother, Lowell, engage in some classic sibling squabbling–"Mom, he's kicking me!"

Lowell, seven, received an autism diagnosis much earlier, at 16 months. Their mom, Page, can recall how different the diagnostic process was for her two children. With Lowell, it was a snap. With Frances, she says, they went from doctor to doctor and were told to simply watch and wait–or that there were various physical reasons for her delays, such as not being able to see well because of an eye condition called strabismus that would require surgical treatment at 20 months. "We got a lot of different random little diagnoses," she recalls. "They kept saying, 'Oh, you have a girl. It's not autism.'"

In fact, the criteria for diagnosing autism spectrum disorder (ASD)–a developmental condition that is marked by social and communication difficulties and repetitive, inflexible patterns of behavior–are based on data derived almost entirely from studies of boys. These criteria, Pelphrey and other researchers believe, may be missing many girls and adult women because their symptoms look different. Historically the disorder, now estimated to affect one out of every 68 children in the U.S., was thought to be at least four times more common in boys than in girls. Experts also believed that girls with autism were, on average, more seriously affected–with more severe symptoms, such as intellectual disability. Newer research suggests that both these ideas may be wrong.

Many girls may, like Frances, be diagnosed late because autism can have different symptoms in females. Others may go undiagnosed or be given diagnoses such as attention-deficit/hyperactivity disorder (ADHD), obsessive-compulsive disorder (OCD) and even, some researchers believe, anorexia. As scientists study how this disorder plays out in girls, they are confronting findings that could overturn their ideas not only about autism but also about sex and how it both biologically and socially affects many aspects of development. They are also beginning to find ways to meet the unique needs of girls and women on the spectrum.

It's Different For Girls

Scientists in recent years have investigated several explanations for autism's skewed gender ratio. In the process, they have uncovered social and personal factors that may help females mask or compensate for the symptoms of ASD better than males do, as well as biological factors that may prevent the condition from developing in the first place [*see "The Protected Sex" on p. 110*]. Research has also revealed bias in the way the disorder is diagnosed.

A 2012 study by cognitive neuroscientist Francesca Happ of King's College London and her colleagues compared the occurrence of autism traits and formal diagnoses in a sample of more than 15,000 twins. They found that if boys and girls had a similar level of such traits, the girls needed to have either more behavioral problems or significant intellectual disability, or both, to be diagnosed. This finding suggests that clinicians are missing many girls who are on the less disabling end of the autism spectrum, previously designated Asperger's syndrome.

In 2014 psychologist Thomas Frazier of the Cleveland Clinic and his colleagues assessed 2,418 autistic children, 304 of them girls. They, too, found that girls with the diagnosis were more likely to have low IQs and extreme behavior problems. The girls also had fewer (or perhaps less obvious) signs of "restricted interests"—intense fixations on a particular subject such as dinosaurs or Disney films. These interests are often a key diagnostic factor on the less severe end of the spectrum, but the examples used in diagnosis often involve stereotypically "male" interests, such as train timetables and numbers. In other words, Frazier had found further evidence that girls are being missed. And a 2013 study showed that, like Frances, girls typically receive their autism diagnoses later than boys do.

Pelphrey is among a growing group of researchers who want to understand what biological sex and gender roles can teach us about autism—and vice versa. His interest in autism is both professional and personal. Of his three children, only his middle child is typical. Kenneth, Pelphrey jokes, has classic "middle-child syndrome" and complains that his siblings "get away with murder because they can blame it on their autism."

Pelphrey is now leading a collaboration with researchers at Harvard University, the University of California, Los Angeles, and the University of Washington to conduct a major study of girls and women with autism, which will follow participants over the course of childhood through early adulthood. The researchers want "every bit of clinical information we can get because we do not know what we ought to be looking for," Pelphrey says. Consequently, they are also asking participants and family members to suggest areas of investigation because they know firsthand what is most helpful and most problematic.

Girls in the study will be compared with autistic boys, as well as typically developing children of both sexes, using brain scans, genetic testing and other measures. Such comparisons can help researchers tease out which developmental differences are attributable to autism, as opposed to sex, as well as whether autism itself affects sex differences in the brain and how social and biological factors interact in producing gender-typical behaviors.

Already Pelphrey is seeing fascinating differences in autistic girls in his preliminary research. "The most unusual thing we keep finding is that everything we thought we knew in terms of functional brain development is not true," he says. "Everything we thought was true of autism seems to only be true for boys." For example, many studies show that the brain of a boy with autism often processes social information such as eye movements and gestures using different brain regions than a typical boy's brain does. "That's been a great finding in autism," Pelphrey says. But it does not hold up in girls, at least in his group's unpublished data gathered so far.

Pelphrey is discovering that girls with autism are indeed different from other girls in how their brain analyzes social information. But they are not like boys with autism. Each girl's brain instead looks like that of a typical boy of the same age, with reduced activity in regions normally associated with socializing. "They're still reduced relative to typically developing girls," Pelphrey says, but the brain-activity measures they show would not be considered "autistic" in a boy. "Everything we're looking at, brain-wise, now seems to be following that pattern," he adds. In short, the brain of a girl with autism may be more like the brain of a typical boy than that of a boy with autism.

A small study by Jane McGillivray and her colleagues at Deakin University in Australia, published in 2014, provides behavioral evidence to support this idea. McGillivray and her colleagues compared 25 autistic boys and 25 autistic girls with a similar number of typically developing children. On a measure of friendship quality and empathy, autistic girls scored as high as typically developing boys the same age—but lower than typically developing girls.

Pelphrey is finding that autism also highlights normal developmental differences between girls and boys. Sex hormones, he says, "affect just about every structure you might be interested in and just about every process you might be interested in." Although boys generally mature much later than girls do, the differences in brain development appear to be quite big—far larger than the differences in behavior.

Masking Autism

Jennifer O'Toole, an author and founder of the Asperkids Web site and company, was not diagnosed until after her husband, daughter and sons were found to be on the spectrum. On the outside, she looked pretty much the opposite of autistic. At Brown University, she was a cheerleader and sorority girl whose boyfriend was the president of his fraternity.

But inside, it was very different. Social life did not come at all naturally to her. She used her formidable intelligence to become an excellent mimic and actress, and the effort this took often exhausted her. From the time she started reading at three and throughout her childhood in gifted programs, O'Toole studied people the way others might study math. And then, she copied them—learning what most folks absorb naturally on the playground only through voracious novel reading and the aftermath of embarrassing gaffes.

O'Toole's story reflects the power of an individual to compensate for a developmental disability and hints at another reason females with autism can be easy to miss. Girls may have a greater ability to hide their symptoms. "If you were just judging on the basis of external behavior, you might not really notice that there's anything different about this person," says University of Cambridge developmental psychopathologist Simon Baron-Cohen. "It relies much more on getting under the surface and listening to the experiences they're having rather than how they present themselves to the world."

O'Toole's obsessive focus on reading and finding rules and regularities in social life is far more characteristic of girls with autism than boys, clinical experience suggests. Autistic boys sometimes do not care whether they have friends or not. In fact, some diagnostic guidelines specify a disinterest in socializing. Yet autistic girls tend to show a much greater desire to connect.

In addition, girls and boys with autism play differently. Studies have found that autistic girls exhibit less repetitive behavior than the boys do, and as the 2014 findings from Frazier and his colleagues suggest, girls with autism frequently do not have the same kinds of interests as stereotypical autistic boys. Instead their pastimes and preferences are more similar to those of other girls.

Frances Pelphrey's obsession with Disney characters and American Girl dolls might seem typical, not autistic, for example. O'Toole remembers compulsively arranging her Barbie dolls. Furthermore, although autism is often marked by an absence of pretend play, research finds that this is less true for girls.

Here, too, they can camouflage their symptoms. O'Toole's behavior might have seemed like typical make-believe to her parents because she staged Barbie weddings just like other little girls. But rather than imagining she was the bride, O'Toole was actually setting up static visual scenes, not story lines.

Also, unlike in boys, the difference between typical and autistic development in girls may lie less in the nature of their interests than in its level of intensity. These girls may refuse to talk about anything else or take expected conversational turns. "The words used to describe women on the spectrum come down to the word 'too,'" O'Toole says. "Too much, too intense, too sensitive, too this, too that."

She describes how both her sensory differences–she can be overwhelmed by crowds and is bothered by loud noise and certain textures–and her social awkwardness made her stand out. Her life was dominated by anxiety. Speaking broadly of people on the spectrum, O'Toole says, "There is really not a time when we're not feeling some level of anxiety, generally stemming from either sensory or social issues."

As she grew up, O'Toole channeled her autistic hyperfocus into another area to which culture frequently directs women: dieting and body image, with a big dollop of perfectionism. "I used to have a spreadsheet of how many calories, how many grams of this, that and the other thing [I could eat]," she says. The resulting anorexia became so severe that she had to be hospitalized when she was 25.

In the mid-2000s researchers led by psychiatrist Janet Treasure of King's College London began to explore the idea that anorexia might be one way that autism manifests itself in females, making them less likely to be identified as autistic. "There are striking similarities in the cognitive profiles," says Kate Tchanturia, an eating disorder researcher and colleague of Treasure's at King's College London. Both people with autism and those with anorexia tend to be rigid, detail-oriented and distressed by change.

Furthermore, because many people with autism find certain tastes and food textures aversive, they often wind up with severely restricted diets. Some research hints at the connection between anorexia and autism: in 2013 Baron-Cohen and his colleagues gave a group of 1,675 teen girls–66 of whom had anorexia–assessments measuring the degree to which they had various autism traits. The research found that women with anorexia have higher levels of these traits than typical women do.

No one is suggesting that the majority of women with anorexia also have autism. A 2015 meta-analysis by Tchanturia and her colleagues puts the figure at about 23 percent–a rate of ASD far higher than that seen in the general population. What all of this suggests is that some of the "missing girls" on the spectrum may be getting eating disorder diagnoses instead.

Further, because autism and ADHD often occur together–and because people diagnosed with ADHD tend to have higher levels of autism traits than typical people do–girls who seem easily distracted or hyperactive may get this label, even when autism is more appropriate. Obsessive-compulsive behavior, rigidity and fear of change also occur in both people with autism and those with OCD, suggesting that autistic females might also be hidden in this group.

Double Standards

Even when young women are comparatively "easy" to diagnose, they still face many challenges in the course of development–particularly social ones. This was the case for Grainne. Her mother, Maggie Halliday, had grown up in a large Irish family and could see early on that her third child, Grainne, was different. "I knew from when she was a couple of months old that there was something not right,"

Halliday says. "She didn't like to be held or cuddled. She could make herself a dead weight and just–you couldn't pick her up."

Although Grainne's IQ tests are in the low normal range, the results do not capture either her abilities or her disabilities well. Today the teenager's intense interests are boy bands and musical theater. Despite being extremely shy, she blooms on stage and loves to sing. "The play she's in, when they deliver the script, within a week, she has everybody's part memorized and every song in the score memorized," Halliday says.

Because of a genetic condition, Grainne is short: 47–and a half, she insists. And although she is laconic and does not tend to initiate conversation, she is also bubbly and smiles frequently, clearly interested in connecting. She weighs what she does say very carefully. For example, when asked whether she thinks autistic girls are more social than boys with autism, Grainne says, "Some might be," not wanting to generalize.

Of course, adolescence is difficult for most kids, but it is especially challenging for autistic girls. Many can cope with the far simpler world of elementary school friendships, but they hit a wall with the "mean girls" of junior high and the subtleties of flirting and dating. Moreover, puberty involves unpredictable changes such as breast development, mood swings and periods–and there are few things that autistic people hate more than change that occurs without warning. "She would like to have a boyfriend–that's why she loves the boy bands," says Halliday, adding that she thinks Grainne may not understand what such a relationship would really mean.

Unfortunately, the autistic tendency to be direct and take things literally can make affected girls and women easy prey for sexual exploitation. O'Toole herself was the victim of an abusive relationship, and she says the problem is "endemic" among women on the spectrum, particularly because so many are acutely aware of their social isolation. "When you feel you're too difficult to love, you'll love for crumbs," she says.

In this way, autism may be more painful for women. Autistic people who do not seem interested in social life probably do not obsess about what they are missing—but those who want to connect and cannot are tormented by their loneliness. A study published in 2014 by Baron-Cohen and his colleagues found that 66 percent of adults with the milder form of ASD (so-called Asperger's) reported suicidal thoughts, a rate nearly 10 times higher than that seen in the general population. The proportion was 71 percent among women, who made up about one third of the sample.

Until very recently, few resources have been available to help autistic girls through these difficulties. Now researchers and clinicians are starting to fill these gaps. For example, Rene Jamison, an assistant clinical professor at the University of Kansas Medical Center, runs a program in Kansas City called Girls Night Out. Aimed at helping affected girls navigate adolescence, it focuses on specific issues such as hygiene and dress. Although this emphasis might seem trivial or a concession to gender stereotypes, in fact, failing to address such "superficial" concerns can cause serious life problems and restrict independence.

Even many highly intelligent girls on the spectrum have difficulties with washing their hair, wearing deodorant and dressing appropriately, Jamison says. Some of this behavior is linked to sensory issues; other aspects of the problem are related to difficulty following the appropriate sequence of behavior when doing something you think is unimportant. "When Grainne was in seventh grade, I had to tell her it was against the law not to wear a bra," Halliday says of her daughter, who found bras uncomfortable. Grainne also did not want to wear deodorant—saying, almost certainly accurately, that the boys smelled worse.

The Girls Night Out group does fun activities, ranging from having manicures to playing sports. Typical girls who get school credit for volunteering provide mentoring and talk about boys and other issues the girls might not want to discuss with adults. "One of the things that we really work on is getting them to try new things to figure out what they might like," Jamison says.

In New York City, Felicity House, which its founders tout as the world's first community center for women on the spectrum, opened in 2015. Funded by the Simons Foundation, it occupies several floors of a spectacular Civil War–era mansion near Gramercy Park and offers classes and social events so autistic women can get to know and support one another. Five of the autistic women who helped to found Felicity House met a few weeks before it opened to talk about life on the spectrum. Only two had been diagnosed as children—one with Asperger's and another with what she said was "ADHD with autistic tendencies." Of the other three women, two had struggled with depression before their diagnosis as adults.

Emily Brooks, 26, is a writer studying for her master's in disability studies at City University of New York. She identifies as gender queer and believes gender norms cause many problems for people on the spectrum. She noted, to broad agreement, that boys are allowed far greater leeway to deviate from social expectations. "If a guy does something that is considered socially inappropriate ... his friends may sometimes encourage some of those behaviors," she said, adding that "teen girls will shut you down if you do anything that's different."

Leironica Hawkins, an artist who has created a comic book about Asperger's, also has to contend with social cues about race. "It's not just because I'm a woman on the spectrum. I'm a black woman on the spectrum, and I have to deal with social cues that [other] people can afford to ignore," she said. She added that she thought women "are probably punished more for not behaving the way we should. I've always heard women are socially aware to the needs of others, and that's not me, most of the time ... I feel like I get pressured to be that way."

Because of these expectations, there is less tolerance for unusual behavior—and not just in high school. Many of the women report having difficulty keeping—but not getting—jobs, despite excellent qualifications. "You can see that in a faculty meeting even at the high-level academic departments," Yale's Pelphrey says. "The guys still get away with much, much more."

As awareness of autism grows, women and girls are already increasingly likely to be diagnosed; this generation clearly has significant advantages over those past. But much more research will need to be done to design better and more gender-appropriate diagnostic tools. Perhaps in the interim, the experiences of women with autism should teach us to be more tolerant of socially inept behavior in women—or less tolerant of it in men. Either way, it is clear that a greater understanding of autism in girls is needed to recognize this condition. And in the process it could illuminate new facets of typical behavior and the way that gender shapes the social world.

The Protected Sex

Simon Baron-Cohen, a professor of developmental psychopathology and director of the University of Cambridge's Autism Research Center, has helped develop several of the major theories that are guiding current thinking about autism. One of these hypotheses, which he is continuing to test, is the "extreme male brain" theory, which first appeared in the literature in 2002. The idea is that autism is caused by fetal exposure to higher than normal levels of male hormones, such as testosterone. This occurrence shapes a mind that is more focused on "systemizing" (understanding and categorizing objects and ideas) than "empathizing" (considering social interactions and other people's perspectives).

In other words, autistic minds may be stronger in areas where male brains, on average, tend to have strengths—and weaker in areas where females, again, speaking broadly, are the superior sex. (When it comes to individuals, of course, these averages do not say anything about a particular man or woman's ability or capacity—nor do the differences necessarily reflect immutable biology rather than culture.)

Numerous recent studies have supported Baron-Cohen's idea. In 2010 he and his colleagues found that male fetuses exposed to higher levels of testosterone in amniotic fluid during pregnancy tend to grow up to have more autism traits. A 2013 study he co-authored, led by his Cambridge colleague Meng-Chuan Lai, found that the brain-scan differences seen in children with autism occurred most often in regions that tend to vary by gender in typical children.

In 2015 Baron-Cohen and his colleagues published results of an analysis of a large group of amniotic fluid samples from Denmark that are linked to population registries of mental health. They found that in boys, having an autism diagnosis was linked with higher levels of fetal testosterone and various other hormones, but the first cohort tested had too few girls with autism, so they are analyzing later births to see if the same results will be found. Further evidence came from a large Swedish study, also published last year, that found a 59 percent increased risk of giving birth to a child with autism among women with polycystic ovary syndrome–an endocrine disorder involving elevated levels of male hormones.

Few scientists–including Baron-Cohen–think that the extreme male brain theory is the whole story. A second idea emerges when looking at the typical strengths of women. If having female hormones and a female-type brain structure increases the ability to read the emotions of others and makes social concerns more salient, it might take a greater number of genetic or environmental "hits" to alter this capacity to the level where autism would be diagnosed. This idea is known as the "female protective" hypothesis.

Along these lines, several studies have shown that in families with affected daughters, there are higher numbers of mutations known as copy-number variations than there are in families where only boys are affected. A 2014 study by geneticist Sbastien Jacquemont of the University of Lausanne in Switzerland and his colleagues found that there was a 300 percent increase in harmful copy-number variants in females with autism, compared with males.

If either–or both–of these hypotheses is correct, then there will always be more boys than girls on the spectrum. "I imagine that once we're very good at recognizing autism in females, there will still be a male bias," Baron-Cohen says. "It just won't be as marked as four to one. It might be more like two to one." –M.S.

Referenced

Thinking in Pictures: My Life with Autism. Expanded edition. Temple Grandin. Vintage, 2006.

Aspergirls: Empowering Females with Asperger Syndrome. Rudy Simone. Jessica Kingsley Publishers, 2010.

The Autistic Brain: Thinking across the Spectrum. Temple Grandin and Richard Panek. Houghton Mifflin Harcourt, 2013.

Sisterhood of the Spectrum: An Asperger Chick's Guide to Life. Jennifer Cook O'Toole. Jessica Kingsley Pub, 2015.

Seeking Precise Portraits of Girls with Autism. Somer Bishop in *Spectrum*. Published online October 6, 2015. https://spectrumnews.org/opinion/seeking-precise-portraits-of-girls-with-autism

The Lost Girls. Apoorva Mandavilli in *Spectrum*. Published online October 19, 2015. https://spectrumnews.org/features/deep-dive/the-lost-girls

About the Author

Maia Szalavitz is the author of, most recently, Undoing Drugs: The Untold Story of Harm Reduction and the Future of Addiction. *She is a contributing opinion writer for the* New York Times *and author or co-author of seven other books.*

The Hidden Potential of Autistic Kids

By Rose Eveleth

When I was in fifth grade, my brother Alex started correcting my homework. This would not have been weird, except that he was in kindergarten—and autistic. His disorder, characterized by repetitive behaviors and difficulty with social interactions and communication, made it hard for him to listen to his teachers. He was often kicked out of class for not being able to sit for more than a few seconds at a time. Even now, almost 15 years later, he can still barely scratch out his name. But he could look at my page of neatly written words or math problems and pick out which ones were wrong.

Many researchers are starting to rethink how much we really know about autistic people and their abilities. These researchers are coming to the conclusion that we might be underestimating what they are capable of contributing to society. Autism is a spectrum disease with two very different ends. At one extreme are "high functioning" people who often hold jobs and keep friends and can get along well in the world. At the other, "low functioning" side are people who cannot operate on their own. Many of them are diagnosed with mental retardation and have to be kept under constant care. But these diagnoses focus on what autistic people cannot do. Now a growing number of scientists are turning that around to look at what autistic people are good at.

Researchers have long considered the majority of those affected by autism to be mentally retarded. Although the numbers cited vary, they generally fall between 70 to 80 percent of the affected population. But when Meredyth Edelson, a researcher at Willamette University, went looking for the source of those statistics, she was surprised that she could not find anything conclusive. Many of the conclusions were based on intelligence tests that tend to overestimate disability in autistic people. "Our knowledge is based on pretty bad data," she says.

This hidden potential was recently acknowledged by Laurent Mottron, a psychiatrist at the University of Montreal. In an article in the November 3 issue of *Nature*, he recounts his own experience working with high-functioning autistic people in his lab, which showed him the power of the autistic brain rather than its limitations. Mottron concludes that perhaps autism is not really a disease at all—that it is perhaps just a different way of looking at the world that should be celebrated rather than viewed as pathology.

Having grown up with two autistic brothers—Alex, four years younger than I, and Decker, who is eight years younger—Mottron's conclusion rings true. As I watched them move through the public schools, it became very clear that there was a big difference between what teachers expected of them and what they could do. Of course, their autism hindered them in some ways—which often made school difficult—yet it also seemed to give them fresh and useful ways of seeing the world—which often don't show up in the standard intelligence tests.

That is because testing for intelligence in autistic people is hard. The average person can sit down and take a verbally administered, timed test without too many problems. But for an autistic person with limited language capability, who might be easily distracted by sensory information, this task is very hard. The most commonly administered intelligence test, the Wechsler Intelligence Scale for Children (WISC) almost seems designed to flunk an autistic person: it is a completely verbal, timed test that relies heavily on cultural and social knowledge. It asks questions like, "What is the thing to do if you find an envelope in the street that is sealed, addressed and has a new stamp on it?" and "What is the thing to do when you cut your finger?"

This year Decker was kicked out of a test much like WISC. Every three years, as he moves through the public school system, his progress is re-evaluated as a part of his Individualized Education Plan—a set of guidelines designed to help people with disabilities reach their educational goal.

This year, as part of the test, the woman delivering the questions asked him, "You find out someone is getting married. What is an appropriate question to ask them?"

My brother's answer: "What kind of cake are you having?"

The proctor shook her head. No, she said, that's not a correct answer. Try again. He furrowed his brow in the way we have all learned to be wary of–it is the face that happens before he starts to shut down–and said, "I don't have another question. That's what I would ask." And that was that. He would not provide her another question, and she would not move on without one. He failed that question and never finished the test.

A test does not have to be like this. Other measures, like Raven's Progressive Matrices or the Test of Nonverbal Intelligence (TONI), avoid these behavioral and language difficulties. They ask children to complete designs and patterns, with mostly nonverbal instructions. And yet they often are not used.

The average child will score around the same percentile for all these tests, both verbal and nonverbal. But an autistic child will not. Isabelle Soulieres, a researcher at Harvard University, gave a group of autistics both WISC and the Raven test to measure the difference between the two groups. Although she expected a difference, she was surprised at just how big the gap was. On average, autistic students performed 30 percentile points better on the Raven test than on WISC. Some kids jumped 70 percentile points. "Depending on which test you use, you get a very different picture of the potential of the kids," she says. Other studies have confirmed this gap, although they found a smaller jump between tests.

The "high functioning" autistic children, with the least severe version of the disability, were not the only ones to score higher. Soulieres conducted a study recently at a school for autistic children considered intellectually disabled. Using the Raven test, she found that about half of them scored in the average range for the general population. "Many of those who are considered low-functioning–if you give them other intelligence tests, you will find hidden potential," she says. "They can solve really complex problems if you give them material that they can optimally process."

What this means, she says, is that schools are underestimating the abilities of autistic children all across the spectrum. The widespread use of the WISC in schools has helped set expectations of autistic kids too low—assuming that they will not be able to learn the same things that the average child can. Based on the test results, people come to the conclusion that autistic children cannot learn, when perhaps they do not learn the same way other people do.

The hidden potential of autistic people seems to fall in common areas—tasks that involve pattern recognition, logical reasoning and picking out irregularities in data or arguments. Soulieres describes working with an autistic woman in her lab who can pick out the slightest flaws in logic. "At first, we argue with her," Soulieres laughs, "but almost each time, she's right, and we're wrong."

Recognizing these talents, rather than pushing them aside to focus on the drawbacks of autism, could benefit not just autistic people, but everyone else as well. Mottron chronicles how much better his science got by working with his autistic lab partner. I got far higher marks on my homework than I would have without Alex, even though his corrections were sometimes infuriating. And many think their potential extends beyond science to all professions, if given the right chances.

Just because a test says someone has potential, that does not mean it is easy to realize. My brother Decker's teachers are convinced—and the tests confirm—that he has hidden potential. But in class, he often falls behind when trying to listen to instructions and gets frustrated when trying to catch up. "It doesn't mean that it's easy for them in everyday life, or that it's easy for their parents or teachers," Soulieres says. "But it shows that they have this reasoning potential, and maybe we have to start teaching them differently and stop making the assumption that they won't learn."

More and more people are starting to wonder what gems might lie hidden in the autistic brain. And if my brothers are any indication, if we keep looking, we will find them.

About the Author

Rose Eveleth is a writer and producer who explores how humans tangle with science and technology. She's the creator and host of Flash Forward, *a podcast about possible (and not so possible) futures, and has covered everything from fake tumbleweed farms to million dollar baccarat heists.*

Autism's "Island of Intactness"

By Darold A. Treffert

My first introduction to autism was a rather jarring one. It was my first day on my child psychiatry rotation. The Department was in a house on the University Hospitals campus in Madison. As I approached the house I heard a very loud "thump! thump! thump!" sound, which literally rattled the rafters of the house.

Inside was a 12-year-old non-verbal, severely autistic girl banging her head on a school desk. She had a helmet on, but even that was not enough to muffle that awful sound.

It occurred to me then that somewhere inside that girl, troubled as she was, had to be some "island of intactness," some uninjured element of reality and wellness, however hidden and deeply buried.

After my residency training I was given the responsibility of starting a Children's Unit at Winnebago Mental Health Institute near Oshkosh, Wisconsin. There were nearly 800 patients at Winnebago at that time and about 25 of them were age 18 or younger. We gathered them together and started the unit. We hired a staff and started a school.

As I looked at those 25 patients, some severely affected, I was reminded of the girl with the helmet. It seemed to me then, as it does now many years later, that somewhere in these patients, often deeply hidden and buried, is that still uninjured "island of intactness." Our task, and opportunity, is to find that hidden spark of wellness. Having discovered it, we need to tend it, love it nourish it, reward it, strengthen it and celebrate it. As we do that, the sliver of un-impairment expands and with it comes improved language, socialization and daily living skills. That results in more independence eventually.

Sometimes, although certainly not always, that bit of intactness is an "island of genius." We call that savant syndrome and I have had the privilege of meeting a number of these extraordinary people. More often, the island of intactness is less spectacular, but nonetheless a valuable discovery.

There are a number of approaches to children with autism these days–Applied Behavioral Analysis (ABA); Son Rise; Rapid Prompting Method (RPM); Early Start Denver Model, to name a few. But embedded in all of them, in my view, is the same, corresponding search for, and then promotion of, the island of intactness. Those methods may use varying techniques–reward, play, relationship building, conversation, socialization, role playing etc.–but the goal of all of them is to discover, engage and grow that sliver toward recovery.

It is this search for strengths, however hidden, that results in progress in treating autistic children. But that same principle of a search for the island of intactness applies in many other conditions as well. In the patient with Alzheimer's disease, for example, we look for preserved memory or skills. So often, traces of musical memory remain, or maybe card playing ability or drawing. We seize on those and tend them, reward them, and celebrate them as a hook into their intactness as a way of interacting still, preserving abilities and even seeing some progress in preserving memory. The same principle applies in the depressed or psychotic patients: we seek to find that bit of reality and health still present, and build on it just as we do with an autistic youngster.

The island of intactness is found in many forms. In one of my Winnebago patients it was the ability to put jigsaw puzzles together, picture side down, just from the shapes of the pieces. Another patient was fascinated with prime numbers and other types of mathematic problems. In a number of other patients, the Ipad has released a torrent of "talk," betraying the myth that children who are mute have nothing to say.

There are many, many other well known examples.

For Owen Suskind, whose father, Ron, made the movie about him called *Life, Animated*, the island of intactness was his passion for Disney movies, which he memorized by the dozens.

Another man, Stephen Wiltshire can draw an entire city, building by building and window by window after a 45-minute helicopter ride. Mute as a child, his first word was "paper." An observant teacher gave him a piece of paper and crayons and his island of intactness, once tapped, unleashed his lifelong astonishing drawing ability. Now he has his own gallery in London.

As a very young child, Leslie Lemke would pluck out rhythms and primitive tunes on his bedsprings; his mother, May, got him a little piano. Now he composes his own pieces.

Ping Lian Yeak went shopping one day with his father He had some ice cream in a brightly colored paper wrapper. When he got home, Ping Lian Yeak studied intently and then reproduced the intricate coloring on the wrapper. His mother recognized that spark of talent, trained it and now Ping Lian Yeak has his own gallery in Malaysia and will exhibit at the Agora Gallery in New York City in March, 2017.

The reward, from the therapist or Mom or Dad, can be a "good job" compliment, a high five, a tummy tickle, a ride in a wagon or a tasty treat. Success breeds success and the journey of discovery, expansion and transition is on.

The search for the island of intactness should always focus on strengths and abilities, not deficits or disabilities. Strength based, individualized approaches, whatever the method or name, once the island of intactness is found, work well with a wide variety of persons whatever the particular condition underlying. Watching those islands of intactness broaden over time, as a conduit of actualization, can give a deep sense of satisfaction for the therapist, whatever the method. But more importantly the improvement can be source of deep relief, and hope, for the patient and family.

The views expressed are those of the author(s) and are not necessarily those of Scientific American.

About the Author

Darold A. Treffert, a psychiatrist, met his first savant in 1962 and continues research on savant syndrome at the Treffert Center in Fond du Lac, Wis. He was a consultant for the 1988 movie Rain Man *and maintains a Web page at www.savantsyndrome.com, hosted by the Wisconsin Medical Society.*

Autism and the Social Mind

By Peter Mundy

Since the modern era of research on autism began in the 1980s, questions about social cognition and social brain development have been of central interest to researchers. This year marks the 20th anniversary of the first annual meeting of the International Society for Autism Research (INSAR), and it is evident in this year's meeting that the growth of social-cognitive neuroscience over the past two decades has significantly enriched autism science. For those unfamiliar with the term, social-cognitive neuroscience is the study of the brain systems that are involved in the causes and effects of social behaviors and social interaction. Some of these involve brain systems involved in thinking about other people's thoughts or intentions, empathizing, social motivation and the impact of social attention on an individual's thinking and emotions.

At the same time, research with and for autistic people has also enriched social-cognitive neuroscience and the understanding of how our social minds develop. Autism spectrum disorder (ASD) is a complex and heterogeneous part of the human condition, or neurodiversity. It is associated with a wide range of life outcomes, from "disorder" or the profound challenges that encumber about 30 percent of affected individuals with minimal language and intellectual disability, to "differences" among people who have well-above-average abilities and accomplishments.

Regardless of their outcomes, though, people on the autism spectrum travel a different path of social-cognitive neurodevelopment that appears to begin in infancy. For example, many experience some level of difficulty with social-cognitive mentalizing, also known as "theory of mind"—the mental representation of other people's thoughts, perspectives, beliefs, intentions or emotions, which enables us to understand or predict their behaviors.

Social-cognitive neuroscience tells us that brain systems of the medial frontal cortex, temporal cortex and parietal cortex, as well as reward centers of the brain, enable mentalizing. Accordingly, differences in the development and/or transmissions of information across this distributed social-cognitive brain network may contribute to differences in mentalizing among autistic people. These differences can lead to a range of outcomes, from problems in the capacity to mentalize to alterations in the spontaneous use of mentalizing, or the motivation and effort involved in mentalizing during social interactions.

These observations are informative, but do not address fundamental questions about how social-cognitive brain systems develop or why their development might be different for autistic people. These questions are essential in autism science because understanding the early course of social-cognitive neurodevelopment may afford the best opportunity to mitigate the profoundly negative effects that social-cognitive differences can have on some autistic people. Serendipitously, this motivation to understand the very early development of our social brain can inform the broader understanding of social-cognitive neuroscience and human nature. As it turns out, one key to understanding the development of our social brains may come from observations of social attention in infancy.

As early as six to 12 months of age, some infants who go on to receive an autism diagnosis already display differences in the development of social attention. They look less frequently at the face and eyes of people than other infants and are less likely to coordinate their attention with another person to adopt a common point of view or reference, or "joint attention." Infants with neurotypical development follow the gaze direction or gesture of other people or lead the gaze of other people to establish joint attention and share information through a common perceptual perspective.

Developing the ability to coordinate attention socially is important in and of itself. For example, every teacher's admonition to students to "pay attention!" is really a request to "pay attention to what I [the teacher] am attending to." Joint attention is vital to social competence at all ages. Adolescents and adults who cannot follow, initiate or join with the rapid-fire changes of shared attention in social interactions may be impaired in their capacity for relatedness and relationships.

Equally important, joint attention is also an early building block of social-cognitive mentalizing. Every time infants coordinate attention socially with other people, they practice perceptual perspective-taking. They do this hundreds if not thousands of times in early development; it tunes aspects of social-brain development that subsequently support the capacity for mental perspective-taking. Mental perspective-taking is synonymous with mentalizing and our ability to understand the thoughts, beliefs, and intentions of other people. Indeed, several studies provide evidence of a significant overlap in brain systems involved in joint attention and social-cognitive mentalizing.

Accordingly, differences in early social attention are thought to contribute to differences in the neurodevelopment of social-cognitive mentalizing in some to many people with autism. Research also suggests that differences in systems that regulate the motivation for social attention might play a role in this aspect of the development of autism, though the nature of this motivation is not understood. One possibility is that decreased motivation to attend to faces may lead to critical early difference in social attention.

Alternatively, differences in the "eye-contact effect" may impact social attention development. The eye-contact effect is a phenomenon in which awareness of being the object of others' attention triggers an arousal response that enhances stimulus salience and information processing during social attention coordination. When we are aware of other people looking at us, changes occur in our mental processes that can benefit social learning. Several studies now suggest that people with autism may be less responsive to, or less aware of, being the object of attention of others.

Hence, autism science raises the hypothesis that the first step toward human social neurocognitive development may involve months of practice with social attention coordination with caregivers during infancy. Moreover, our response to eye contact of other people may provide an early motivational stance that prioritizes infant social attention development and the development of our social brains. Notably, recent studies indicate that imitating the behavior of young children with autism, which likely affects a child's awareness that another person is looking at them, can improve joint attention and language development.

Of course, the most fundamental lesson we can draw from all these observations about the development of our social mind is that we are all more similar than different, regardless of our paths of neurodevelopment, and that autistic people have much to teach us about the nature of human nature.

This is an opinion and analysis article.

Referenced

Baron-Cohen, S. (2019). The concept of neurodiversity is dividing the autism community. *Scientific American*.

Chevallier, C., Kohls, G., Troiani, V., Brodkin, E. S., & Schultz, R. T. (2012). The social motivation theory of autism. *Trends in cognitive sciences*, 16(4), 231-239.

Gulsrud, A. C., Hellemann, G., Shire, S., & Kasari, C. (2016). Isolating active ingredients in a parent mediated social communication intervention for toddlers with autism spectrum disorder. *Journal of Child Psychology and Psychiatry*, 57(5), 606-613.

Grynszpan, O., Bouteiller, J., Grynszpan, S., Le Barillier, F., Martin, J. C., & Nadel, J. (2019). Altered sense of gaze leading in autism. *Research in Autism Spectrum Disorders*, 67, 101441.

About the Author

Peter Mundy, Ph.D., is the president of the International Society for Autism Research (INSAR) and professor and Lisa Capps Endowed Chair of neurodevelopmental disorders and education in the School of Education and the Department of Psychiatry and Behavioral Sciences at the University of California, Davis (UC Davis). He is also director of educational research at the UC Davis MIND Institute.

Making Eye Contact Signals a New Turn in a Conversation

By Lydia Denworth

What is found in a good conversation? It is certainly correct to say words—the more engagingly put, the better. But conversation also includes "eyes, smiles, the silences between the words," as the Swedish author Annika Thor wrote. It is when those elements hum along together that we feel most deeply engaged with, and most connected to, our conversational partner, as if we are in sync with them.

Like good conversationalists, neuroscientists at Dartmouth College have taken that idea and carried it to new places. As part of a series of studies on how two minds meet in real life, they reported surprising findings on the interplay of eye contact and the synchronization of neural activity between two people during conversation. In a paper published on September 14 in *Proceedings of the Natural Academy of Sciences USA*, the researchers suggest that being in tune with a conversational partner is good but that going in and out of alignment with them might be better.

Making eye contact has long been conceived as acting like a cohesive glue, connecting an individual to the person with whom they are talking. Its absence can signal social dysfunction. Similarly, the growing study of neural synchrony has focused on the positive aspects of alignment in brain activity between individuals.

In the new study, by using pupil dilation as a measure of synchrony during unstructured conversation, psychologist Thalia Wheatley and graduate student Sophie Wohltjen found that the moment of making eye contact marks a peak in shared attention—and not the beginning of a sustained period of locked gazes. Synchrony, in fact, drops sharply after looking into the eyes of your interlocutor and only begins to recover when you and that person look away from each other. "Eye contact is not eliciting synchrony; it's disrupting it," says Wheatley, senior author of the paper.

Why would this be? Conversation requires some level of synchrony, but Wheatley and lead study author Wohltjen speculate that breaking eye contact ultimately propels the conversation forward. "Perhaps what this is doing is allowing us to break synchrony and move back into our own heads so that we can bring forth new and individual contributions to keep the conversation going," Wohltjen says.

"It's a fantastic study," says psychiatrist and social neuroscientist Leonhard Schilbach of the Max Planck Institute of Psychiatry in Munich, who studies social interaction but was not involved in the research. He applauds the design of the experiment to replicate natural encounters and the focus on free-form conversation. The results suggest, he says, that "interpersonal synchrony is an important aspect of social interactions but may not always be desirable."

Others in the field are drawn to the researchers' creative way of thinking about conversation, which is described as "a platform where minds meet" in the paper. "Such a conceptualization may inspire other researchers to think about conversation differently and study it more deeply," says Juliana Schroeder, a social psychologist at the Haas School of Business at the University of California, Berkeley, who also was not involved in the research.

The new work builds on an earlier study by Wheatley and psychologist Olivia Kang, now at Harvard University, who showed that pupillary synchrony serves as a measure of shared attention. Our pupils get larger and smaller as a reflexive response to changes in light but also, to a lesser degree, when we are physiologically aroused. Kang and Wheatley tracked eye movements in speakers as they recounted positive or negative memories about their life. Then the researchers tracked the eye movements of people listening to the same stories at a later point in time. They found that the pupil dilation of the listeners synchronized to that of the speakers when there were emotional peaks in the stories. "We knew this was a marker of people being on the same page as each other," Wheatley says.

For the current paper, Wohltjen wanted to extend those earlier findings by studying face-to-face conversation in order to see how eye contact might influence shared attention in real time. She put 186 psychology students at Dartmouth, all relative strangers, into conversational pairs and asked them to talk for 10 minutes about anything they wanted while she tracked their eye movements. Participants also watched videos of their conversations and rated their remembered level of engagement minute by minute.

"We expected that eye contact worked like a cattle prod to get two people back onto the same wavelength," Wohltjen says. If that were so, the onset of eye contact should have led to a subsequent increase in pupillary synchrony. Instead the researchers found the opposite: a peak in synchrony at the onset followed by a decrease. But they also found that participants reported being more engaged when they were making eye contact. "We thought, 'Perhaps this making and breaking of eye contact must do something to help the conversation,'" Wohltjen says.

Previous studies of eye contact have generally been passive, as in Wheatley and Kang's earlier work. The real-world design of Wohltjen's experiment served as a reminder that most people naturally look at and away from each other many times during a conversation. Holding someone's gaze for too long—or not at all—can seem awkward. As the researchers thought further about what eye contact might be doing for us, they turned to the literature on creativity. There they recognized the constraints of too much synchrony. "If people are trying to innovate in some way, you don't want people in lockstep with each other," Wheatley says. "You want people to [say], 'What if we did this? What if we did that?' You need people to be providing their independent insights and building that way."

The idea that eye gaze can be used to modulate synchrony is intriguing to other researchers. "The elegant experimental approach [in this paper] might be helpful to quantitatively investigate psychiatric conditions, which can be described as 'disorders of social interaction,'" says Schilbach, who has studied gaze and other elements of social interaction in autism.

The findings also help explain the frustrations of Zoom and other video conferencing platforms, on which real eye contact is nearly impossible to make—or break—because of the positioning of cameras and windows on screens. (The paper's publication prompted a lively discussion of just that phenomenon on Twitter.)

Wheatley can imagine follow-up studies that examine a variety of conversational contexts. How does the dynamic dance between making and breaking synchrony play out when a parent is instructing a child, for instance? Presumably, in that situation, a parent would be hoping for the child's full attention and therefore complete synchrony. On the other hand, perhaps the study helps explain why long car rides, in which people do not look at each other the whole time, are often conducive to deep conversation.

"There might be an optimal sweet spot in this coupling, decoupling thing—where people are really listening to each other, but they're also fueling the conversation with new ideas," Wheatley says. "Those conversations might be the most fun."

About the Author

Lydia Denworth is a Brooklyn, N.Y.–based science writer and a contributing editor for Scientific American. *She wrote about the neuroscience of stuttering in our August 2021 issue. She is co-author of* Parent Nation.

Autism Might Slow Brain's Ability to Integrate Input from Multiple Senses

By Katherine Harmon

Children with autism often focus intently on a single activity or feature of their environment. New research might help to explain this behavioral trend, providing evidence that the brains of young people with autism are slower to integrate input coming from more than one sense at the same time.

During study of the disorder decades ago, research into these basic tendencies was common. But in subsequent years, scientists have tended to focus more on complex issues, ranging from communication troubles to underlying genetic patterns.

Recently, however, more studies have set their sights back on some of the simple processes that most people take for granted, such as sensory intake, as a way to better understand more high-level manifestations, such as social interaction issues. "We believe that these things interact in very significant ways," says Sophie Molholm, an associate professor of neuroscience at Albert Einstein College of Medicine and co-author of a new study about multi-sensory processing.

The research, published online August 19 in *Autism Research*, used electroencephalograms (EEGs) to measure electrical activity in the brain through the scalp of subjects as they encountered various stimuli. Seventeen children (ages six to 16 years) with autism—and 17 age- and IQ-matched normally developing kids—watched a silent video of their choice throughout the testing. Meanwhile, tones and vibrations were administered in random order, sometimes separately, sometimes at the same time. The EEG readings were time-stamped to the stimuli and compared across all of the children to assess brain activity trends during single- and multi-sensory stimulation. Although the video presented visual stimuli, Molholm points out that because it was a consistent exposure throughout the experiments and the EEG readings were set to pick up on the sound and somatosensory stimuli and averaged out over so many tests, it becomes akin to "background brain activity that will sum to zero," she notes. "It's really just something to keep them busy."

A simple stimulus takes about 20 milliseconds to arrive in the brain. When information from multiple senses registers at the same time, integration takes about 100 to 200 milliseconds in normally developing children. But those with autism took an average of 310 milliseconds to integrate the noise and vibration when they occurred together.

This difference, "at one level, is a very minor time delay," Molholm says. "But if you're thinking about human cognition... that could really interfere with normal processing," making what she describes as a "pretty significant impact." The research team also found that shortly after a stimulus was presented, brain activity in which timing seemed similar in typically developing children and in those with autism, the children with autism had lower overall signal strength, signified by lower amplitude waves on the EEG.

Although the study cannot definitively explain any direct behavioral correlates, it might hint at some of the underlying reasons for many of the disorder's hallmarks, such as sensitivity to excessive sensory stimulation.

"Maybe part of the reason these children might want to block out this—what seems to them extraneous stimulation—[is that] it fails to gain meaning for them as it does for other people," Molholm notes. She and her colleagues made clear in their study that these children were still eventually able to integrate the inputs from multiple senses and that there is a chance that as they become older, the children's integration speed could increase. The researchers proposed that one reason for this consistent delay is that children with autism might need to direct their attention to stimuli to achieve integration, whereas most others are capable of doing it implicitly.

Although the EEG is able to detect brain activity location and timing on a relatively minute scale, it does not paint a complete picture of the physiology behind these observed delays. "This is just a small step to understand multi-sensory integration," Molholm says. "Part of what we'd like to do next is look at brain anatomy and possibly how connectivity between different functional regions differs in autism."

Pinning down more data about how children with autism respond to multi-sensory stimuli should also help researchers, therapists and parents to evaluate sensory-integration therapy, which has been a popular treatment for individuals with autism. At present, "there's no objective measure to know if your sensory-integration therapy has worked," Molholm notes.

Empirical EEG maps might also eventually become a component of a more precise diagnostic toolbox, Molholm says. "We'd certainly like that to be the case," she says. And the EEG-stimulus test has the advantage of being "a passive paradigm," in which children do not have to execute tasks or take many directions, thus allowing most all developmental levels and a wide range of ages to undergo parallel analysis.

Section 5: Myths and Misconceptions

Autism: An Epidemic?

By Scott O. Lilienfeld and Hal Arkowitz

If the figure of "one in 166" has a familiar ring, perhaps that's because you recently heard it on a television commercial or read it in a magazine. According to widely publicized estimates, one in 166 is now the proportion of children who suffer from autism. This proportion is astonishingly high compared with the figure of one in 2,500 that autism researchers had accepted for decades. Across a mere 10-year period—1993 to 2003—statistics from the U.S. Department of Education revealed a 657 percent increase in the nationwide rate of autism.

Not surprisingly, these bewildering increases have led many researchers and educators to refer to an autism "epidemic." Representative Dan Burton of Indiana also declared in 2001 that "we have an epidemic on our hands." But what's really going on?

Before we explore this question, a bit of background is in order. Autism is a severe disorder that first appears in infancy. Individuals with autism are characterized by problems in language, social bonding and imagination. All suffer from serious communication deficits, and some are mute. They do not establish close relationships with others, preferring to remain in their own mental worlds. They engage in highly stereotyped and repetitive activities, exhibiting a marked aversion to change. About two thirds of autistic individuals are mentally retarded. For reasons that are unknown, most are male.

As a consequence, investigators have turned to environmental factors for potential explanations. The causal agents proposed include antibiotics, viruses, allergies, enhanced opportunities for parents with mild autistic traits to meet and mate, and, in one recent study conducted by Cornell University researchers, elevated rates of television viewing in infants. Few of these explanations have been investigated systematically, and all remain speculative.

Problem Shots?

Yet one environmental culprit has received the lion's share of attention: vaccines. At first blush, vaccines would seem to make a plausible candidate for the source of the epidemic. The debilitating symptoms of autism typically become apparent shortly after age two, not long after infants have received vaccinations for a host of diseases. Indeed, many parents claim that their children developed autism shortly after receiving inoculations, either following a vaccine series for mumps, measles and rubella (German measles)—the so-called MMR vaccine—or following vaccines containing thimerosal, a preservative containing mercury.

Much of the hype surrounding a vaccine-autism link was fueled by a widely covered investigation of 12 children published in 1998 by British gastroenterologist Andrew Wakefield and his colleagues. The study revealed that symptoms of autism emerged shortly after the children received the MMR vaccine. (Ten of the 13 authors have since published a retraction of the article's conclusions.) Public interest in the vaccine-autism link was further stoked by the provocatively titled book *Evidence of Harm* (St. Martin's Press, 2005), written by investigative journalist David Kirby, which was featured in an extended segment on NBC's *Meet the Press*.

Yet recently published research has not been kind to the much ballyhooed vaccine-autism link. The results of several large American, European and Japanese studies demonstrate that although the rate of MMR vaccinations has remained constant or declined, the rate of autism diagnoses has soared. In addition, after the Danish government stopped administering thimerosal-bearing vaccines, the rates of autism continued to rise. These studies and others, summarized by the Institute of Medicine, suggest there is little evidence that vaccines cause autism. It is possible that vaccines trigger autism in a small subset of children, but if so that subset has yet to be identified.

Changing Criteria

Making matters more confusing, ample reason exists to question the very existence of the autism epidemic. Vaccines may be what scientists call an "explanation in search of a phenomenon." As University of Wisconsin–Madison psychologists Morton Ann Gernsbacher and H. Hill Goldsmith and University of Montreal researcher Michelle Dawson noted in a 2005 review, there is an often overlooked alternative explanation for the epidemic: changes in diagnostic practices. Over time the criteria for a diagnosis of autism have loosened, resulting in the labeling of substantially more mildly afflicted individuals as autistic.

Indeed, the 1980 version of the American Psychiatric Association's diagnostic manual (*DSM-III*) required individuals to meet six of six criteria for an autism diagnosis. In contrast, the 1994 version (*DSM-IV*), which is currently in use, requires individuals to meet any eight of 16 criteria. Moreover, whereas *DSM-III* contained only two diagnoses relevant to autism, the *DSM-IV* contains five such diagnoses, including Asperger's syndrome, which most researchers regard as a high-functioning variant of autism.

Legal changes may also be playing a significant role. As Gernsbacher and her colleagues noted, an amended version of the Individuals with Disabilities Education Act (IDEA), passed by Congress in 1991, required school districts to provide precise counts of children with disabilities. IDEA resulted in sharp surges in the reported numbers of children with autism. Nevertheless, these numbers are not based on careful diagnoses of autism or on representative samples of the population. As a consequence, researchers who rely on "administrative-based estimates," which come from government data submitted by schools, will arrive at misleading conclusions about autism's prevalence. They must instead rely on "population-based estimates," which are developed from statistically reliable and representative surveys of autism's occurrence in the general population.

Referenced

Separating Fact from Fiction in the Etiology and Treatment of Autism: A Scientific Review of the Evidence. J. D. Herbert, I. R. Sharp and B. A. Gaudiano in *Scientific Review of Mental Health Practice*, Vol. 1, No. 1, pages 23–43; Spring–Summer 2002.

The Prevalence of Autism. E. Fombonne in *Journal of the American Medical Association*, Vol. 289, No. 1, pages 87–89; 2003.

Immunization Safety Review: Vaccines and Autism. Immunization Safety Review Committee. Board of Health Promotion and Disease Prevention, Institute of Medicine. National Academy Press, 2004.

Three Reasons Not to Believe in an Autism Epidemic. M. A. Gernsbacher, M. Dawson and H. H. Goldsmith in *Current Directions in Psychological Science*, Vol. 14, pages 55–58; 2005.

About the Authors

Scott O. Lilienfeld and Hal Arkowitz serve on the board of advisers for Scientific American Mind. *Lilienfeld is a psychology professor at Emory University, and Arkowitz is a psychology professor at the University of Arizona.*

We Need to Stop Moving the Goalposts for Autism

By Darold A. Treffert

How many children have "autism"? Is that number increasing? Is there an "epidemic" of autism or have we merely been continually refining it, expanding it and moving the goalposts since it was first described by Leo Kanner in 1943?

I met my first child with autism in 1959, almost 60 years ago. I had the good fortune to learn about autism firsthand from Kanner himself, when he was a visiting professor at the University of Wisconsin Medical School and I was a medical student there.

Then, in 1962, I started a Children's Unit at Winnebago Mental Health Institute in Wisconsin, on which almost all the children were autistic. That's also the unit on which I met my first savant.

The question of autism prevalence engaged me even then. In 1970, I carried out the first U.S. study of the epidemiology of infantile autism, published in *Archives of General Psychiatry*. Actually, autism was then most commonly diagnosed formally as childhood schizophrenia.

At that time, the Wisconsin Department of Health and Human services provided me with a printout listing all patients age 12 and under seen for evaluation or treatment and given a diagnosis of childhood schizophrenia between fiscal 1962 and 1967 in 30 community mental health and child guidance clinics; four state and county mental hospitals; three colonies and training schools; and the children's treatment center, children's diagnostic center and university hospitals.

I found 280 unduplicated cases, representing a prevalence of autism of 3.1 cases per 10,000 children ages 3–12 in Wisconsin. Interestingly, as a validation, a 1966 study by Lotter in the county of Middlesex, United Kingdom in 1966 found a prevalence of autism of 4.8 cases per 10,000 children. Admittedly this study has some serious limitations, which make the prevalence figure for autism artificially low. But it stands in stark contrast to the prevalence of one child in 59 with a diagnosis of autism in the 2018 Centers for Disease and Control and Prevention report (which uses 2014 data). That report found 168 children per 10,000 instead of 3.1 per 10,000 in my 1970 study. Which of those two divergent figures is closest to being correct? And how did the figure get that divergent?

The CDC Report

When the report came out, the headlines read along the lines of "Autism cases continue to rise: now 1 in 59 children have autism." But let's look at that CDC study more critically. It is based on an active surveillance system established in 2000 that estimates autism spectrum disorder (ASD) among children age 8 years living in 11 states.

Using that system, the prevalence of autism (ASD) rose from 1 in 150 children in 2000–2002, to 1 in 68 children during 2010–2012 and 1 in 59 children in 2014. That means the prevalence of autism more than doubled in the 12-year period between 2000 and 2012 and increased nearly 16 percent just in the two-year period between 2012 and 2014.

That is preposterous. From 1 per 150 children to 1 per 59 children with autism in slightly more than a decade? No wonder headlines speak of an "epidemic." Are these believable figures, or might it be because we keep diluting the condition and expanding the definition, and in so doing we keep moving the goalposts? I believe that to be the case.

There are problems that cast doubt on that method and those numbers for actual prevalence of ASD. Figures include "educational autism," which is a diagnosis made by teachers or educational specialists in the classroom and "medical autism," based on review of available medical records. There are no actual in-person evaluations. Casting more doubt is the fact that the prevalence in one state, Arkansas, was 1.31 percent but more than double that in another, 2.93 percent in New Jersey. The prevalence in Wisconsin rose 31 percent between 2012 and 2014. Is that a believable actual increase in ASD in two years in Wisconsin?

I don't think so. From my perspective as an observer of "autism" for over 60 years, I do believe there is an actual increase in the number of cases of autistic disorder, but it is not an epidemic. And it has not been an increase of 31 percent in two years here in Wisconsin, for example, or a more than 150 percent increase in the U.S. in the past decade. That is simply not believable. Instead much of that "epidemic" is a dilution of the rigor of the criteria for autism.

That may make interesting headlines, increased awareness, expanded insurance coverage or benefit fund raising, but it is not an accurate assessment of the actual prevalence of autism. Recently several leading heart organizations changed the definition of 'hypertension" from 140 systolic over 90 diastolic to 130/80. Instantly the number of Americans with high blood pressure jumped 14 percentage points from 32 percent to 46 percent.

Call Things by Their Right Names

There are many reasons why the diagnosis of autism needs to be precise. Labeling some children as autistic when they have other learning disorders such as hyperlexia or language delay, for example, or "educational autism," alarms families unnecessarily and can result in the wrong intervention or educational placement, which happens particularly with children who read early or speak late. Even "blindisms"–repetitive self-comforting behaviors such as rocking in children with visual impairments–can be mistaken for autism. As elsewhere in medicine, the first step in treatment is to make the correct diagnosis.

But my concern goes beyond that. I believe that autism is a group of disorders, rather than a single disorder, just as mental retardation or dementia represent groups of conditions rather than single ones. I also believe that one day, as we sort autism into its component parts, we will be able to identify the subgroups with the same precision as we do phenylketonuria with a diaper or blood test or trisomy 21 or fragile x with a chromosome test.

But the less precise and broader the diagnosis becomes, the less chance we have of finding subgroups among increasingly heterogeneous, diluted diagnostic groups. There is a proliferation now of metabolic, enzyme, imaging and brain wave tests or chromosome determinations that hold promise for detecting autism with the precision of the diaper test, trisomy 21 or fragile X.

To do that we need to call things by their right names both clinically and research-wise, and the present method of assessing prevalence in the U.S. is not doing that well since we keep moving the goalposts.

Others share that view. In a *Scientific American* essay this month titled "Is It Time to Give Up on a Single Diagnostic Label for Autism?" Simon Baron-Cohen states: "But the main argument against a single diagnostic label is that the inclusion of subtypes will likely lead to greater scientific progress in understanding the precise causes of the heterogeneity, and greater translational progress in understanding what kinds of intervention and support are needed, and for whom." I would add the prospect of prevention to that list of possibilities.

The search for a reliably consistent measure of autism prevalence continues outside the U.S., as well.

A 2017 article in the *Universal Journal of Clinical Medicine* shows a 2012 global median autism prevalence figure of 17/10,000 or 1 in 588 for autistic disorder and 62/10,000 or 1 in 161 for all pervasive developmental disorders. That is at some considerable variance from the 1 in 59 figure in the U.S. One of the important remaining tasks in the search is to bring the American Psychiatric Association's *DSM-V* definition of autistic spectrum disorder in line with the definition in the World Health Organization's *International Classification of Diseases–Eleventh Revision* (*ICD-11*). They're still inconsistent.

If that happens, of course, the goalposts may move again.

The views expressed are those of the author(s) and are not necessarily those of Scientific American.

About the Author

Darold A. Treffert, a psychiatrist, met his first savant in 1962 and continues research on savant syndrome at the Treffert Center in Fond du Lac, Wis. He was a consultant for the 1988 movie Rain Man *and maintains a Web page at www.savantsyndrome.com, hosted by the Wisconsin Medical Society.*

Desperation Drives Parents to Dubious Autism Treatments

By Nancy Shute

When Jim Laidler's oldest son, Benjamin, was diagnosed with autism, he and his wife started looking for help. "The neurologists were saying, 'We don't know what causes autism, and we don't know what the outcome for your son will be,'" Laidler relates. "No one was saying, 'Here's what causes it; here's what treats it.'"

But when the Laidlers, who live in Portland, Ore., searched the Web, they found dozens of "biomedical" treatments that promised to improve or even cure Benjamin's inability to talk, interact socially or control his movements. So the parents tried them on their son. They began with vitamin B6 and magnesium, the nutritional supplements dimethylglycine and trimethylglycine, vitamin A, gluten- and casein-free diets, the digestive hormone secretin, and chelation, a drug therapy designed to purge the body of lead and mercury. They applied the purported treatments to Benjamin's little brother, David, who also was diagnosed with autism. Chelation did not seem to help much. Any effect from secretin was hard to tell. The diets showed promise; the Laidlers hauled special food with them everywhere. And Mom and Dad continued to feed the boys dozens of supplements, calibrating doses up and down with every change in behavior.

The first sign that their experiments had failed came when Laidler's wife, who had become increasingly skeptical, quit giving Benjamin supplements. She waited two months before telling her husband. Her silence ended the day Benjamin grabbed a waffle off a buffet during a family trip to Disneyland and wolfed it down. The parents watched with horror, convinced that he would regress the instant he went off his restricted diet. He didn't.

Jim Laidler should have known better. He is an anesthesiologist. He was aware from the beginning that the treatments he was using on his children had not been tested in randomized clinical trials, the gold standard for medical therapies. "At first I tried to resist," he says. But hope won out over skepticism.

Hundreds of thousands of parents every year succumb to the same desire to find something—anything—that might alleviate the symptoms of their struggling sons and daughters: lack of speech and communication, inept social interactions, repetitive or restrictive behaviors such as hand flapping or fixating on objects. As many as 75 percent of autistic children are receiving "alternative" treatments not developed by conventional medicine, according to some studies. And yet the therapies are often bogus. They have not been tested for safety or effectiveness, they can be expensive, and some of them may actually do harm. Fortunately, recent spikes in autism diagnoses and parent activism are pushing more federal and private funding toward research that could someday yield scientifically proved results.

No Cause, No Cure

The demand for autism treatments is rising largely because more children are being diagnosed under broader criteria. Back in the 1970s, when autism was called "infantile psychosis"—a mix of social deficits and mental retardation—the condition was considered rare. Pediatricians would tell parents who were worried that, say, their eight-month-old wasn't making eye contact, to wait and see.

Studies indicated that about five children in 10,000 had autism, but the rate grew higher when doctors redefined the condition as autism spectrum disorder, which included milder symptoms. By the time an updated version of psychiatry's bible, the *Diagnostic and Statistical Manual of Mental Disorders*, known as the *DSM*, was published in 1994, doctors had added Asperger's syndrome—a high-functioning form popularized in the movie *Rain Man*—and a catchall group termed "pervasive developmental disorder, not otherwise specified." Doctors also started realizing the benefits of early diagnosis and treatment. In 2007 the American Academy of Pediatrics recommended universal screening of all children for autism between 18 and 24 months. By then, the autism rate had shot up to one in 110 children.

Whether greater diagnoses reflect a true rise in cases is a matter of controversy, because little is known about what causes the condition. "For the large majority of people with autism, we don't even know a clear-cut genetic factor," says David Amaral, research director of the MIND Institute at the University of California, Davis, and president of the International Society for Autism Research. No biomarkers are available to tell which children are at risk or to gauge how well treatments work. The greatest body of research is on behavioral interventions designed to teach social interaction and communication, which appear to help some children to varying degrees.

The lack of empirically vetted therapies makes it far easier for sellers of untested treatments to market hope. "What you've got is a combination of pseudoscience and fraud," says Stephen Barrett, a retired psychiatrist in Chapel Hill, N.C., who reports on dubious medical treatments at his Web site Quackwatch.com. "Parents are under a great deal of stress. They so want their kid to be better. They see improvement over time, and they give credit to the wrong thing." Those gains are not because of the "treatment," he says, but because children mature as they age.

Snake-oil salesmen litter the Web. One site tells parents they can "defeat the autism in your child" by buying a $299 book; another touts a video of "an autistic girl improving after receiving stem cell injections." Many parents acknowledge that they get their information from the Internet, and "a lot of parents rely on anecdotal reports, friends or other parents," says Brian Reichow, an associate research scientist at the Yale Child Study Center. "In autism, the research has not caught up with the treatments."

Hope doesn't come cheap, either. Alternative treatments such as lying in a pressurized, hyperbaric oxygen chamber (used to overcome compression sickness), which temporarily increases blood oxygen levels, cost $100 an hour or more, with one to two hourly sessions recommended daily. Sensory integration therapy, which can range from wrapping children in blankets or placing them in a hug machine to having them play with scented clay, can cost up to $200 an hour. Purveyors charge as much as $800 an hour for consultations and thousands more for vitamins, supplements and lab tests. Parents in an ongoing survey by the Interactive Autism Network at the Kennedy Krieger Institute in Baltimore report spending an average of $500 a month out-of-pocket. The one treatment for autism that has been proved to be somewhat effective–behavioral therapy–can also be the most expensive, at $33,000 or more a year. Although state early-intervention programs and public school districts often cover these costs, the wait for free evaluations and services can be long. All told, direct medical and nonmedical costs for autism add up to an average of $72,000 a year, according to the Harvard School of Public Health.

Medical Snake Oil

Unproved therapies extend to medications. Some practitioners prescribe drugs approved for other illnesses. The compounds include Lupron, which blocks the body's production of testosterone in men and estrogen in women; it is used to treat prostate cancer and to "chemically castrate" rapists. Doctors also have prescribed the diabetes drug Actos and intravenous immunoglobulin G, usually used for leukemia and pediatric AIDS. All three medications have serious side effects and have never been tested for safety or efficacy in autism.

Chelation, the primary treatment for lead poisoning, is another legitimate medical therapy turned autism "cure." The drug converts lead, mercury and other metals into chemically inert compounds that the body can excrete in urine. Some people think exposure to such metals, particularly the ethylmercury used as a preservative in vaccines, can cause autism, even though no studies have demonstrated such a link. Indeed, autism diagnosis rates continued to climb after ethylmercury was phased out of most vaccines in 2001. Chelation can cause kidney failure, particularly in the intravenous form favored for autism. In 2005 a five-year-old boy in Pennsylvania with autism died after being given intravenous chelation.

Concern led the National Institute of Mental Health to announce plans in 2006 for a randomized, controlled trial of chelation for autism. But the institute shelved the study in 2008 because officials could find "no clear evidence for direct benefit," and the treatment put the children at "more than a minimal risk." Their worry arose in part from lab studies that showed cognitive problems in rats that received chelation and did not have metal poisoning. "I don't think anybody had much faith that chelation would be the answer for a large number of children," says Thomas R. Insel, director of the NIMH. His researchers, he adds, are "more interested in testing medications that have a mechanistic basis."

Predictably, the abandoned study fueled charges that Big Science was ignoring alternative treatments. Money has always flowed more to discovering cures that work than to discrediting ones that don't. Until very recently, most autism research has been conducted in the social sciences and special education fields, where research budgets are modest and protocols are far different than medicine's. At times only a single child is involved in a study. "We would not even call it evidence," says Margaret Maglione, associate director of the Southern California Evidence-Based Practice Center at RAND, who is leading a federally funded review of behavioral treatments that will be published in 2011.

Many Haystacks, Few Needles

State-of-the-art scientific research simply does not exist for many autism treatments, and where it does, the number of people studied is often small. In 2007 the Cochrane Collaboration, an independent evaluator of medical research, reviewed casein- and gluten-free diets, which are based on the premise that compounds in casein, a milk protein, and in gluten, a wheat protein, interfere with receptors in the brain. Cochrane identified two very small clinical trials, one with 20 participants and one with 15. The first study found some reduction in autism symptoms; the second found none. A new, randomized, controlled trial of 14 children, reported this past May by Susan Hyman, an associate professor of pediatrics at the University of Rochester School of Medicine and Dentistry, found no changes in attention, sleep, stool patterns or characteristic autistic behavior. "Slowly the evidence is starting to accumulate that [diet] is not the panacea people are hoping for," says Susan E. Levy, a pediatrician at Children's Hospital of Philadelphia who has evaluated the evidence with Hyman.

Levy has firsthand experience with the level of effort needed to sway public opinion. Secretin became a hot commodity after a 1998 study reported that three children had better eye contact, alertness and use of expressive language after being given the hormone during a diagnostic procedure for gastrointestinal problems. Media outlets, including *Good Morning America* and *Ladies' Home Journal*, recounted parents' joyous tales of children transformed. The National Institute of Child Health and Human Development rushed to fund clinical trials. By May 2005 five randomized clinical trials had failed to reveal any benefit, and interest in secretin waned. It took years for that to play out, says Levy, who helped conduct several of the trials: "Research is very labor-intensive, and progress may be slow." Parents may feel helpless, she adds, and "they don't want to leave any stone unturned."

The good news is that rising demand for proved treatments is attracting money for research. When the first International Meeting for Autism Research was held in 2001, barely 250 people attended. This past May 1,700 researchers, graduate students and parent advocates showed up for the meeting in Philadelphia. New technologies and increased public awareness have helped make autism a more appealing research focus. And in the mid-1990s parents began adopting the sophisticated lobbying and fund-raising tactics used for AIDS and breast cancer, leaning on foundations and the federal government.

As a result, in the past decade U.S. research funding for autism has increased by 15 percent a year, with an emphasis on clinical applications. The National Institutes of Health allocated $132 million for autism work in 2009, with an additional $64 million from the American Recovery and Reinvestment Act, much of which is being earmarked to develop patient registries and other investigative tools. Private foundations, including the Simons Foundation and Autism Speaks, contributed $79 million in 2008. According to Autism Speaks, about 27 percent of all funding is being spent on investigating treatments, 29 percent on causes, 24 percent on basic biology and 9 percent on diagnosis.

These new pursuits encompass efforts to find out if early intervention with behavioral therapies that teach children social skills through repetition and reward can be used successfully with children when they are very young, when the brain is in the thick of learning language and social interaction. A study by several universities, released online in November 2009, found that children who were given two years of behavioral therapy for 31 hours a week, starting when they were between 18 and 30 months old, made substantial gains in IQ (17.6 points, compared with 7 points in the control group), and in skills of daily living and language. Seven of the 24 children in the treatment group improved enough that their diagnosis was upgraded from autism to the milder "not otherwise specified" form; only one child in the 24 who were given other interventions was given a milder diagnosis. The Autism Treatment Network has built a registry of more than 2,300 children for research on treatments for medical complications often suffered by autistic children, especially gastrointestinal issues and difficulty sleeping, and it plans to develop guidelines that could be used by pediatricians nationwide.

Toward a True Science of Autism

Efforts to find medications, including those used in other neurological disorders, may have higher hurdles to clear. Medical interventions have been "a bit of a disappointment," Insel says. For example, antidepressants that boost the neurotransmitter serotonin in the brain are very effective in reducing the repetitive hand motions of obsessive-compulsive disorders, but a review by the Cochrane Collaboration reported in August that the drugs did nothing to alleviate the repetitive motions typical of autism. Among the new candidates are a medication that enhances REM sleep, which is lacking in children with autism, and oxytocin, a hormone that promotes childbirth and lactation and is thought to encourage mother-infant bonds. A study published in February by the National Center for Scientific Research in France found that 13 teenagers with Asperger's were better at identifying images of faces after inhaling oxytocin. A big leap would have to be made between that one study and the notion that oxytocin could mitigate autism's most devastating symptoms. Insel says: "We have a lot of work to do."

That work is starting to be done. In June a consortium of researchers who scanned the genes of 996 grade-schoolers found rare, novel genetic variations in children with autism. Some of the glitches affect genes that control communication across synapses–the contact points between neurons in the brain, a key focus of autism inquiries. "The actual mutations are different [among individuals], but there may be some commonalities in the biological pathways," says Daniel Geschwind, a professor of neurology and psychiatry at the David Geffen School of Medicine at U.C.L.A., a study leader. Geschwind is also a founder of the Autism Genetic Resource Exchange database of DNA samples from more than 1,200 families with autism, which was used in the study. Tests to confirm a culprit, or treatments that might fix the glitch, are still years away.

For now, more parents may be choosing not to experiment, if only so they can sleep at night. Michael and Alison Giangregorio of Merrick, N.Y., decided when their son, Nicholas, was diagnosed at age two that they would use only evidence-based treatments such as applied behavioral analysis. "It's difficult enough and challenging enough to help my son," Michael says. "I was not willing to try experimental therapies. I need to do what clinicians and researchers have taken the time to prove works and to prove that it doesn't do any additional harm." Nicholas is now nine, and although he remains nonverbal, behavioral therapy has taught him to use physical signals when he needs to go to the bathroom. He can now wash his hands, sit through dinner in a restaurant and walk down an aisle in the drugstore without flapping his hands. "Obviously, the goal of my family, and most families, is to lead as normal a life as possible," says Michael, a 45-year-old Wall Street trader. "Normal is going out to dinner as a family."

Jim Laidler's path to the same place was far more crooked. Although he embraced alternative treatments for his sons, he also tried to persuade practitioners that they needed to apply the rigor of mainstream science in evaluating such options. "I kept harping on it. Did you do any controls?" he says. His oldest son, now 17, will probably never be able to live on his own, yet his younger son is in a regular middle school. Of the many treatments the family tried, Laidler, 51, says: "This is basically shamanism in a lab coat." Thousands of desperate parents are hoping that science will one day offer stronger medicine.

About the Author

Nancy Shute has covered neuroscience and children's health issues for more than 20 years. She writes the On Parenting *blog for* U.S. News & World Report, *where she is a contributing editor.*

Hyping Autism Research "News" Is a Disservice to People with Autism

By Alycia Halladay

Click-worthy health and science headlines are an essential currency in today's media world. When they pertain to autism, they might include phrases like "groundbreaking trial," "offer hope" or "game-changer." But for people with autism and their families, these headlines and the research news stories they highlight often bring false hope, confusion—or worse.

There is something about autism, a disorder that remains widely misunderstood, that seems to encourage the promulgation of news coverage about potential "breakthroughs" and unorthodox treatment approaches. A nearly constant stream of headlines touts promising new findings that supposedly help explain the origins of autism spectrum disorder (ASD), improve our understanding of its key features or reveal novel ways to treat the symptoms.

This attention is a mixed blessing. It can encourage talented scientists to design research to better understand autism. It also generates support for advocacy efforts and research funding, and I have seen it motivate people to participate in research studies.

However, there is a dark side to this almost insatiable interest in autism science news: it has created an environment that encourages media hype of early, preliminary findings, with headlines that are tantalizing but not always accurate. The hype machine also too often promotes mediocre or even bad science, which ultimately puts people with autism at risk.

In the worst scenarios, families inspired by media coverage may pursue treatments that are both ineffective and unsafe. This has been the case with MDMA, or 3,4-methyldioxymethamphetamine, otherwise known as ecstasy, to treat social anxiety in autistic adults. Much media coverage of this experimental treatment failed to report that the drug is neurotoxic in animal models and humans, and that a "safe" dose has not been established. As a result, the public received complete misinformation via mainstream media outlets. The false hope of MDMA might have led some in the autism community to pursue an illegal—and, more importantly, potentially lethal—intervention.

This wasn't the first such debacle. In 2013, prominent media outlets reported on an autism treatment that entailed consuming worm eggs, then allowing them to grow in the intestines. This therapeutic approach isn't as radical as one might think; it is undergoing rigorous experimentation for treatment of Crohn's disease and colitis. But in reporting positive effects in treating autism, critical details about the study's significant limitations, including its very small sample size and the fact that it was not peer-reviewed, were buried in the last paragraph of one prominent news report.

The coverage led to conversations on autism chat rooms about how to obtain worm eggs and use them at home. In another case, the headline "Stem Cells Offer Hope for Autism" might have encouraged families to travel to international sites with unregulated medical practices to obtain this therapy, which is still unproven. Conversely, the media is largely missing the mark on the potential of medical marijuana, confusing different cannabinoids and mixing up indications in their headlines. This type of misinformation will only serve to stifle badly needed research into phytocannabinoids in marijuana that do, in fact, show promise for treating epilepsy, which commonly co-occurs in children with autism.

The mainstream news media need to consider a more measured and responsible approach to covering autism research. This should include very careful vetting of which studies are reported. Not all scientific journals are equal in their scientific rigor or review policies, so just because a study is "published" does not mean it necessarily has scientific significance.

In other cases, research becomes newsworthy when it is presented at meetings, or when preliminary data are announced in a press release without any review whatsoever. To get a better handle on what information is legitimate and significant, media outlets should partner with autism experts to help decipher what is, in fact, news. This may mean taking a more measured approach to headlines, relying on additional outside sources to provide necessary perspective, and being more explicit with qualifiers about the limitations of the findings being reported. It may also mean scuttling stories based on the cautionary insights of those third-party experts.

Finally, media stories should be updated when later findings either prove or disprove early, headline-making scientific theories—and the updates should be promoted as aggressively as the original stories were. We all deserve to know when these news-making studies fail, have unintended negative consequences or ultimately don't produce the anticipated results.

News coverage of autism science is important for a community constantly searching for answers. Journalists have an obligation to do a better job of making sure those answers are real.

About the Author

Alycia Halladay is the chief science officer at the Autism Science Foundation. She oversees the science programs and portfolio of ASF. She previously served as senior director of environmental and clinical sciences at Autism Speaks. She holds a PhD in psychology from Rutgers University, where she also completed a postdoctoral fellowship in pharmacology and toxicology.

GLOSSARY

accommodations Something done to provide what is needed for someone or something.

attention deficit hyperactivity disorder (ADHD) A brain disorder that affects how you pay attention, sit still, and control your behavior.

cisgender Relating to a person whose sense of personal identity and gender matches their assigned sex at birth.

cognitive Relating to conscious mental activities, such as thinking, understanding, learning, and remembering.

criteria Things used as a reason for making a judgment or decision.

empathy The feeling that you understand and share another person's experiences and emotions.

euthanasia The act of killing someone who is very sick or injured in order to prevent any more suffering.

gender-fluid Relating to a person whose gender identity is not fixed.

heterogeneity The state of consisting of different parts or elements.

neural Relating to or involving a nerve or the nervous system.

neurodivergent Differing in mental function from what is considered typical or normal.

neurotypical Not displaying neurologically atypical patterns of thought or behavior.

paradigm shift An important change that happens when the usual way of thinking about or doing something is replaced by a new way.

prenatal Relating to pregnant women and their unborn babies.

prevalence The degree to which something is common or widely accepted.

savant A person who does not have normal intelligence but who has very unusual mental abilities that other people do not have.

spectrum A complete range of different things.

supersaturate To cause something to have more than it can contain.

symptoms Changes in the body or mind that indicate that a disease is present.

FURTHER INFORMATION

"What is Autism Spectrum Disorder?" Centers for Disease Control and Prevention, March 31, 2022, https://www.cdc.gov/ncbddd/autism/facts.html.

Northwestern University, "When kids' autistic brains can't calm down: Mutation is linked for first time to seizures in autism and is new drug target," *ScienceDaily*, April 5, 2018, https://www.sciencedaily.com/releases/2018/04/180405120316.htm.

Quick, Jonathan D. and Heidi Larson, "The Vaccine-Autism Myth Started 20 Years Ago. Here's Why It Still Endures Today," *Time*, February 28, 2018, https://time.com/5175704/andrew-wakefield-vaccine-autism/.

Rutgers University, "Gene mutation leading to autism found to overstimulate brain cells," *ScienceDaily*, November 21, 2022, https://www.sciencedaily.com/releases/2022/11/221121130748.htm.

Sifferlin, Alexandria, "This May Explain the Rise in Autism Diagnoses," *Time*, January 5, 2015, https://time.com/3652619/autism-diagnosis/.

University of Utah Health, "Gene that guides earliest social behaviors could be key to understanding autism," *ScienceDaily*, November 23, 2022, https://www.sciencedaily.com/releases/2022/11/221123193629.htm.

Wallis, Claudia, "Autism Treatment Shifts Away from 'Fixing' the Condition," *Scientific American,* December 1, 2022, https://www.scientificamerican.com/article/autism-treatment-shifts-away-from-fixing-the-condition/.

Wickelgren, Ingrid, "Is a Diagnostic Test to Blame for Why We Know So Little about Autism in Girls?" *Scientific American*, November 22, 2022, https://www.scientificamerican.com/article/is-a-diagnostic-test-to-blame-for-why-we-know-so-little-about-autism-in-girls/.

CITATIONS

1.1 A New Idea That Could Help Us Understand Autism by Pamela Feliciano (August 6, 2021); 1.2 By the Numbers: Autism Is Not a Math Problem by Ferris Jabr (January 30, 2012); 1.3 The Problem with Asperger's by Edith Sheffer (May 2, 2018); 2.1 Detecting Autism Early by Ulrich Kraft (June 1, 2007); 2.2 Redefining Autism: The New DSM Criteria by Ferris Jabr (January 30, 2012); 2.3 Early Intervention Could Help Autistic Children Learn to Speak by Marissa Fessenden (July 17, 2012); 2.4 On the Brink of Breakthroughs in Diagnosing and Treating Autism by Geraldine Dawson (May 9, 2016); 2.5 Autism Starts Months before Symptoms Appear, Study Shows by Karen Weintraub (February 15, 2017); 2.6 Is It Time to Give Up on a Single Diagnostic Label for Autism? by Simon Baron-Cohen (May 4, 2018); 2.7 We Need Better Diagnostic Tests for Autism in Women by Zhara Astra (April 7, 2022); 2.8 Coming Out Autistic by Brandy Schillace (November 5, 2021); 3.1 What Really Causes Autism by Simon Makin (November 1, 2015); 3.2 The Concept of Neurodiversity Is Dividing the Autism Community by Simon Baron-Cohen (April 30, 2019); 3.3 Clearing Up Some Misconceptions about Neurodiversity by Aiyana Bailin (June 6, 2019); 3.4 The Neurodiversity Movement Should Acknowledge Autism as a Medical Disability by Yuval Levental (July 17, 2019); 3.5 Are Geeky Couples More Likely to Have Kids with Autism? by Simon Baron-Cohen (November 1, 2012); 3.6 How Big Data Are Unlocking the Mysteries of Autism by Wendy Chung (April 30, 2021); 4.1 Autistic People Make Great Social Partners if You Actually Give Them a Chance by Scott Barry Kaufman (March 9, 2020); 4.2 Autism–It's Different in Girls by Maia Szalavitz (March 1, 2016); 4.3 The Hidden Potential of Autistic Kids by Rose Eveleth (November 30, 2011); 4.4 Autism's "Island of Intactness" by Darold A. Treffert (March 8, 2017); 4.5 Autism and the Social Mind by Peter Mundy (May 15, 2021); 4.6 Making Eye Contact Signals a New Turn in a Conversation by Lydia Denworth (September 21, 2021); 4.7 Autism Might Slow Brain's Ability to Integrate Input from Multiple Senses by Katherine Harmon (August 21, 2010); 5.1 Autism: An Epidemic? by Scott O. Lilienfeld and Hal Arkowitz (April 1, 2007); 5.2 We Need to Stop Moving the Goalposts for Autism by Darold A. Treffert (May 24, 2018); 5.3 Desperation Drives Parents to Dubious Autism Treatments by Nancy Shute (October 1, 2010); 5.4 Hyping Autism Research "News" Is a Disservice to People with Autism by Alycia Halladay (November 2, 2018)

Each author biography was accurate at the time the article was originally published.

INDEX